Your Shield and Buckler

Psalm 91:11

Your Shield and Buckler

"His truth shall be thy shield and buckler."

Psalm 91:4

Jorge Diaz

MAIDEN VOYAGE PUBLISHING CO.
SAN CARLOS, CALIFORNIA

Unless otherwise indicated, all Scripture quotations are taken from the *King James Version* of the Bible.

Italics appearing in Scripture quotations have been added by the author for emphasis.

Your Shield and Buckler
First Printing 2002
ISBN 1-931545-03-0
Copyright © 2002 by Jorge Diaz
P.O. Box 246542
Pembroke Pines, FL 33024

Published by Maiden Voyage Publishing Company
www.mvpublishing.com

Cover design by Michael Wech

Contents

Introduction

Sunday, June 22, 1980. I was assigned to the day shift Uniformed Patrol Division and was en route to a domestic disturbance call. The only other information I had been given was that a female was bleeding.

I arrived on the scene along with my backup officer and the sector sergeant. A woman immediately burst out of the home's front door. She was literally covered in her own blood. She told me that her son was high on cocaine and had beaten her.

Moment's later, a second, younger woman ran to the front door shouting, "He's got a gun, he's gonna kill himself!"

She directed the other officers and me through the home and led us to her boyfriend's room. I was the first officer and I remember thinking, *If this were a police television drama, now would be a good time for a commercial break.* But this was not television, and we were not actors. This was real life and, as we would soon discover, real lives were at stake.

I walked through the narrow hallway leading to the subject's room and saw that his bedroom door was slightly ajar. I peered inside and saw a young man clad only in his underwear and seated on the edge of his bed. He held the barrel end of a shotgun under his chin with one hand. His other hand held the stock of the shotgun on the floor with his thumb placed along the trigger. I was certain I was about to see this young man's head explode with a twitch of his thumb.

My first impulse was fear. Next, thoughts of getting out of the house raced through my mind. I began thinking of possible escape routes in the home, and even wondered if I could just blast my own personal exit through a wall. Almost instantly, I remembered that fear has no place in me. "God has not given me the spirit of fear..." I recalled, "...but of power, and of love, and of a sound mind" (2 Timothy 1:7).

I also realized that "no weapon" (that includes shotguns), "formed against *me* shall prosper" (Isaiah 54:17). I prayed these scriptures silently, and immediately felt complete peace come over my mind and inside my spirit.

I knew what spiritual forces were responsible for what was happening around me. I knew that Satan, "the thief," was present in that room, and that his intentions were to "steal, kill, and destroy" as many lives as he could (John 10:10). I knew that I had to bind Satan's spirit of death, so in a hushed voice, I bound him by telling him that he would not be taking this young man's life. I ordered him to release the man in the Name of Jesus (Matthew 18:18, Mark 16:17).

The man maintained his posture with the shotgun in the same position. He had a crazed look on his face and in his eyes. Although I was attempting to communicate with him, he was not responding. I needed God's perfect guidance in this situation and I wanted God's perfect will to take place, so I prayed in the Spirit in a quiet, almost inaudible voice, and then continued speaking with the young man. (John 16:13, Romans 8:26–27).

After a few minutes, the young man began to answer me. Along with telling me his troubles, he repeatedly threatened to "end it all" and kill himself.

Throughout our brief conversation, I had been standing behind a wall in the hallway with my head near the bedroom door's opening. I eventually asked permission to enter the room. The man consented. I pulled up a chair within three feet of the bed and sat down.

I began to witness to his spirit about Jesus and how He and I were present to help him. The man shifted his position by lying down on the bed and placing the barrel end of the shotgun in his mouth. He then wrapped his legs around the stock of the rifle. Moving around nervously, he changed back to his original place on the edge of the bed.

As the man switched positions, Satan spoke to my mind and told me to make a move for the shotgun.

I knew the author of those thoughts was the devil, and I refused to obey him (John 10:5). Eventually, I discovered that this man was six feet, five inches tall and weighed substantially more than my five-foot, ten-inch frame. I praise God for the wisdom to keep this battle in the spiritual arena rather than the natural one.

I was in the room with the young man for approximately forty-five minutes. By now, the shift commander had arrived on the scene along with numerous other officers. Uniformed men and women surrounded the house with their weapons drawn. Fire rescue vehicles and medical personnel were also present in order to treat possible casualties.

As if all these circumstances were not overwhelming enough, it was the height of summer in torrid south Florida, and the house had no air-conditioning. Due to the heat and incredible tension, everyone inside the house was soaked with sweat. I, however, remained cool and dry. I did not perspire as much as one bead of sweat. It was as if an angel were "encamped round about me" (Psalm 34:7).

In conversation with the subject, he shared with me that he was not willing to surrender his shotgun because I was armed. In more than ten years of experience as a police officer, I had been trained *never* to surrender my handgun or disarm myself. However, I was led by the Holy Spirit to provide this man with an unorthodox proposition, an offer I would not have been able to comfortably make based on my own thinking. I told the young man that I would remove my own gun and give it to one of my fellow officers in the hallway if he would give me his gun. Although he expressed that he had some apprehension and distrust toward police officers, the man agreed.

I removed my revolver from its holster and attempted to hand it to one of the officers in the hallway. No one would accept my gun. They, too, had been trained that an officer should never give up his or her weapon. I made it clear that it was *my* intent to disarm myself and that I would be dropping my gun if no officer grabbed it first. I felt one of the officers hesitantly reach out and take my gun from my hand. The man placed the shotgun against the wall, out of my own reach, but still well within his.

My lieutenant entered the bedroom slowly. Startled, the subject hurriedly grabbed his shotgun again and pointed it in the direction of the lieutenant and me. I had so much confidence in God's promises of protection, that the sight of the business end of that shotgun did not move me (2 Corinthians 5:7).

After reminding the man that we had made a deal and that I had kept my part of the bargain, he emptied a live round from the chamber of the shotgun. Every officer present eventually confided in me that hearing the shotgun's racking sound was one of the most frightening moments in each one's careers. They were anticipating a loud blast would follow. Again, I had absolutely no fear or expectation that anyone present would be harmed.

The subject was calmly taken into custody and, in accordance with departmental policy, was transported to a hospital for psychiatric evaluation. Knowing that this was no real, permanent solution, I returned to the home to visit the man, who was allowed to return home after his evaluation. I presented him with a Bible I had purchased for him, and I witnessed to the family at length about Jesus.

A few weeks later, I was patrolling in my police car when someone on a motorcycle pulled alongside me at a traffic light. After briefly staring in my direction, he raised his helmet's face-shield and revealed his identity; it was the young man. Although it was the same physical man I had dealt with, his countenance told a different story. He thanked me for everything I had done. It was thrilling to see his smile and the life that now shone on his face! I gave my heavenly Father all of the glory, all of the credit, and all of the honor for having used me as His vessel to save and change this man's life while insuring the safety of my fellow officers and myself!

This gripping story is the factual account of a situation faced by a great man of God and former Hialeah police officer; a man I consider my spiritual father, and one whom I am eternally thankful to God for, presently retired, Sergeant Terrell Duke.

Sergeant Duke's testimony is one of victory. It exemplifies how every life-threatening situation should end for all Christian peace officers. Sadly, though, many good men and women who were born again and Spirit-filled have died or been seriously injured while carrying out their law enforcement duties. Praise God, those who lost their lives made heaven and we will see them again, but neither death nor injuries were God's *perfect* will for these individuals.

God's perfect will for these officers and for officers today is that they "...not die, but live, and declare the works of the Lord" (Psalm 118:17). His perfect will is that they share with their families and friends the testimony of how God empowered them to defeat the enemy. God's highest and best is that these officers continue to serve and be witnesses unto others, harvesting souls for God's kingdom. God's perfect will is that all of His children lead a full, blessed life on this earth, and go to heaven long after they have retired and have seen even their grandchildren's children!

Many Christians are unaware of the fact that this is God's will for their lives. They are not familiar with the spiritual truths and guarantees that God has provided us as we carry out His plan on the earth. However, a growing number of individuals, those such as Sergeant Duke, are discovering that throughout God's Word are promises of safety and protection for every believer. We are learning that God's Word is also full of spiritual weapons against which no demon in hell or thug on the street can prevail.

This book has not gotten into your hands by accident or coincidence. It was written specifically for *you*. You were created for a very important purpose, and you have a destiny to fulfill. I believe as you read the truths revealed in this book, you will begin to see more of your divine purpose, and how important it is for you to live each day enveloped in the protection God has provided for you. Read on and find out about who you really are in Christ. Discover the divine protection God has afforded you as His child, and learn how to apply these proven, scriptural truths in your own professional and personal life!

CHAPTER 1

Ignorance Destroys

After reading Sergeant Duke's account of one of his many triumphs and victories as a Christian police officer, you might be left wondering why other Christians have not fared as well. You might even ask yourself why men and women, whom you personally knew as wonderful, devout human beings, had a different, possibly tragic outcome.

"Why, God?" has long been our response when tragedy struck one of our own. God's answer is so simple and obvious it saddens me to think that so many Christians, peace officers and civilians alike, are not aware of it. The answer is found in the Book of Hosea, chapter 4, and verse 6:

> **My people are destroyed for lack of knowledge....**

Notice God did not say the "heathen" or the "wicked" are destroyed; God is specifically referring to

His people. Since the time of this scripture's writing, God's people have been and are being destroyed.

God did not use less descriptive words such as "broken" or "injured" to describe the result of a lack of knowledge. Something broken can be salvaged by repair, but when it is destroyed, its existence is irreversibly wiped out.

Some ministers use the term "perish" in that scripture in place of "destroyed." At first glance, perish seems like a more amiable word; however, *perish* means "to die or cease to exist, especially in a violent or untimely manner."[1] This definition illustrates a fittingly graphic consequence. God wants us to understand the reality and poignant truth that remaining ignorant can eventually bring about our destruction: our untimely, premature death.

Proverbs 11:14 supports the same message God conveys to us in Hosea 4:6. It reads in part:

Where no counsel is, the people fall….

Where there is "no counsel"—advice or guidance[2] —God's people fall. The word *fall* in this instance does not mean "stumble" or "trip." The more precise definition is "to drop wounded or dead."[3] What a sad, yet startlingly powerful truth. The Lord has made it clear that *our* lack of knowledge *is* the inherent cause of our untimely destruction.

EARTHLY WISDOM

The lack of knowledge or counsel God is referring to in these scriptures is not the same kind of information we might receive at a university or other training institution. Police officers in general are well educated in all aspects of their profession. When it comes to officer safety, most officers understand the importance of acquiring as much information as possible on the subject. The knowledge we have gained at the police academy and throughout our careers in training seminars and presentations is beneficial and necessary, but this kind of knowledge provides only well-meaning, yet imperfect procedures.

The apostle James explains this type of knowledge as *earthly* wisdom, and refers to it as *sensual* or "based on the physical or natural senses"[4] (James 3:13–16). Such wisdom is limited to our physical faculties and, therefore, does not equip us to cope with unforeseen variables beyond the control of even the best officer survival skills. These variables are factors for which no amount of research and training can prepare us. Even if we do everything by the book, unforeseen contingencies exist which can cause things to go tragically wrong.

A few years ago, a fellow officer and associate of mine, whom I knew to be a Christian, responded to a neighbor dispute call at an apartment building. This officer followed good officer safety habits and so he waited for his backup to arrive before approaching the apartment where the problem tenant was located.

When backup came, both officers walked together to the particular apartment's door and eventually knocked. The officers stood on either side of the door with their backs against the wall, insuring that they did not expose themselves to the doorway. Proper text-book safety procedures were being followed to the letter when, "Bang!" A single gunshot rang out from inside the apartment. The bullet traversed the solid wood door at just the right angle and struck the Christian officer behind the head. He would never regain consciousness and eventually died from the severity of his wound.

My intent is not to judge this man in any way. I knew him personally and was deeply saddened by his predicament. At the time of this incident, I myself lacked the revelation of God's Word that I am blessed with and able to share today. I am merely illustrating that we cannot depend solely on earthly wisdom or the world's knowledge for our safety. Statistics and personal experiences have shown that officers injured or killed in the line of duty often did not make *any* procedural errors.

WISDOM FROM ABOVE

The lack of knowledge God is referring to in Hosea and Proverbs has to do with the wisdom contained in His Word. This wisdom "from above" is "pure, peaceable and gentle" (James 3:17). God's knowledge is perfect and able to bring total harmony, regardless of the circumstances. God's wisdom takes into account every hidden factor—every unknown threat—and overcomes them all!

My purpose in writing this message is to help individuals tap into the wisdom of God that is available in every situation. Developing our spiritual capabilities and walking in the knowledge of God eliminates even freak occurrences and guarantees our victory every time.

Let's look at what our heavenly Father says is in store for the believer who chooses to discover such knowledge.

> **My son, attend to my words; incline thine ear unto my sayings.**
> **Let them not depart from thine eyes; keep them in the midst of thine heart.**
> **For they are *life* unto those that find them, and *health to all their flesh*.**
>
> **Proverbs 4:20–22**

Although the Bible is full of scriptures that emphasize how vital it is to "attend" or "pay attention" to God's Word, Proverbs 4:20–22 boldly declares and guarantees us *life* and *health* if we will attend to His words and receive the wisdom and counsel found in His sayings.

God also tells us to keep His words "in our heart"— our spirit. When we "take something to heart," we accept it as truth in our innermost being. It is *then* that those words will provide us with life and health to keep us from destruction.

PROMISES OF PROTECTION

God didn't stop with only one such promise. The Book of Proverbs is full of scriptures assuring our safety, protection, length of life and deliverance if we will attend to the God-kind of wisdom. I recommend reading and studying all of Proverbs to learn the benefits that are available in every area of life.

The following scriptures pertain specifically to divine protection as a result of obtaining the wisdom of God.

> **But whoso hearkeneth unto me shall *dwell safely*, and shall be quiet from fear of evil.**
> **Proverbs 1:33**

Dwell means "to exist in a given place or condition."[5] In this instance, it implies a condition that is safe and free of fear or distress. Listening to God causes us to live in a peaceful state, away from anxiety, a lack of confidence, or any of the many forms fear can take. We are also to live free from anything evil, harmful, or disastrous.

> **He layeth up sound wisdom for the righteous: he is a *buckler* to them that walk uprightly.**
> **He keepeth the paths of judgment, and preserveth the way of his saints.**
> **Proverbs 2:7–8**

A *buckler* is a round shield with straps that fit around the arm of a foot soldier.[6] Archers and gladiators primarily used bucklers in ancient times. With the use of a buckler, a warrior had his hands free to concentrate on firing his arrows while he was kept safe and protected.

Obtaining God's sound wisdom allows us to concentrate on our tasks, while it keeps us safe from any attack. As our buckler, the Lord preserves and protects us!

> **Discretion shall *preserve* thee, understanding shall *keep* thee:**
> **To *deliver* thee from the way of the evil man, from the man that speaketh froward things.**
> **Proverbs 2:11–12**

God's knowledge—His discretion and understanding—shall preserve us. *Preserve* means "to keep safe, as from injury or peril."[7]

Have you ever had to deal with anyone whose intentions were less than honorable? The knowledge of God's Word also delivers or sets us free and saves us from evil men who attempt to cause us harm.

How long will God's wisdom and discretion preserve us?

> **Hear, O my son, and receive my sayings; and *the years of thy life shall be many.***
>
> **Proverbs 4:10**

> **The fear of the Lord is the beginning of wisdom: and the knowledge of the holy is understanding.**
> **For by me** *(wisdom) thy days shall be multiplied,* **and** *the years of thy life shall be increased.*
>
> **Proverbs 9:10–11**

> **Happy is the man that findeth wisdom, and the man that getteth understanding.**
> *Length of days* **is in her right hand....**
>
> **Proverbs 3:13, 16**

Notice how many times God tells us that His kind of knowledge will insure *long* life for us. When God tells us that attaining His wisdom will lengthen our days, rest assured, He is referring to living well past the completion of a meager twenty- to thirty-year retirement plan.

> She *(wisdom)* is a tree of life to them that lay hold upon her: and happy is every one that retaineth her.
> My son, let not them depart from thine eyes: keep sound wisdom and discretion:
> So shall they be *life unto thy soul*, and grace to thy neck.
> Then shalt thou *walk in thy way safely*, and *thy foot shall not stumble*.
>
> **Proverbs 3:18, 21–23**

God doesn't call wisdom "a tree of existence," He calls wisdom "a tree of *life!*" Anyone can exist day to day and lack life. Think of the number of people we encounter daily who are hungry for peace. They lack spiritually, physically, socially and financially. Having *life* is having everything about us sound and whole; nothing broken, nothing missing. Life in our soul means that our mind and emotions are in perfect health and free of stress. God says that His wisdom guarantees us this highest form of life.

Jesus Himself explained life best when He said, "...I am come that they might have life, and that they might have it more abundantly" (John 10:10). Living an abundant life means having an over-sufficient, plentiful supply of life. We are not only supposed to survive our career as law enforcement officers, we are supposed to come through unharmed and without disfigurement or disability. We are to be totally free from feeling oppressed and discouraged. *That* is life in abundance!

Proverbs 3:23 also promises that even while walking our "beat" or driving our marked unit, God's wisdom keeps us from stumbling or making a wrong decision that would lead to calamity or accidents. This implies an assurance of safety from not only outward attacks, but from self-imposed, destructive mistakes and accidents as well. Since our profession provides us with enumerable opportunities to make such critical errors, this is truly a blessed assurance from God.

Also notice that in Proverbs 3:21, God beckons us to keep His words of wisdom in front of our eyes. God is trying to convey to us the importance of obtaining His knowledge through the study of His Word. Knowing the Word is the only way we will understand God's will and how to walk in His wisdom. It is our responsibility to obtain counsel from God, and to discover what He has made available to us for our protection.

Find your Bible and follow along with each of the following chapters. It is important that you compare the teachings in this book or "training manual" with the scriptures in your own Bible, our main "textbook." Confirm for yourself that the wisdom this book is saturated with is not based on personal beliefs, but is inspired and backed by God's Holy, written Word. Do not allow yourself to be destroyed by a lack of knowledge of God's provisions to keep you safe. Read every sentence as if your life depends upon it— because it does!

CHAPTER 2

True Integrity

The No. 1 defense God has provided for us, His children, is His Word. God repeatedly gives us His literal Word—our shield of defense—insuring safety and protection from harm.

Before we cover many of the verses that pertain to our rights to God's divine protection, it is important that we know how serious God is about what He says in His Word. It is vital for us to appreciate and understand the integrity of God's Word, and how perfectly God adheres to what He says.

One of the earliest examples of God showing us how much He reverences the things He tells us is found in the Book of Numbers:

> **God is not a man, that he should lie; neither the son of man, that he should repent: hath he said, and shall he not do it? or hath he spoken, and shall he not make it good?**
>
> **Numbers 23:19**

Most believers know that God has the power to do anything. However, one thing we can boldly say our omnipotent Father is incapable of doing is lying. God, unlike man, cannot and will not lie. What God says when He speaks to us through His Word is the ultimate source of truth. As John 17:17 says, "...*thy word* is truth."

When someone reads a verse of scripture from the Bible and says to himself, "I just don't think this part of the Bible is true," he is inadvertently calling God a liar.

Few Christians would openly shake their fist toward heaven, and yell, "You are a fraud, God, and I don't believe everything the Bible says!"

Yet privately denying or disagreeing with portions of God's Word is just as damaging. Either God's Word is true, or whatever a person chooses to believe—contrary to God's Word—is true. Both beliefs cannot be true.

The apostle Paul speaks clearly along these lines to the Christians in Rome.

> **For what if some did not believe? Shall their unbelief make the faith of God without effect?**
> **God forbid: yea, let God be true, but every man a liar....**
>
> **Romans 3:3–4**

This scripture also reassures us that God's Word is just as true and effectual whether or not others choose to believe it.

I am reminded of a motorist I stopped one afternoon for committing a traffic violation. His demeanor was, at best, less than admirable. He could not "believe" that I had stopped him for such a "petty" offense. Neither did the driver "believe" that I was writing him a ticket for his infraction.

When he refused to sign the citation, I explained to him that his refusal to sign the summons could result in his arrest. The man then expressed his "disbelief" that a citizen of his caliber could be arrested for such a thing. He adamantly declined to sign the ticket.

Handcuffed and seated in the back seat of my patrol car, the man could not "believe" he was going to jail and that his vehicle was about to be impounded. I am certain this highly dissatisfied customer of the criminal justice system was sitting in his cell that evening in complete denial of the predicament in which he had just placed himself. His "belief" had no effect on the reality of his situation.

Likewise, it is imperative that we submit to the Word of God and maintain a teachable spirit. We should not question or challenge the veracity of God's Word based on what *we* think, or what others—including church leaders—have taught us, if it is not in line with God's ultimate reality.

> ...Hear what God the Lord will speak: for he will speak peace unto his people, and to his saints....
>
> **Psalm 85:8**

> Beware lest any man spoil you through philosophy and vain deceit, after the tradition of men, after the rudiments (*fundamentals*) of the world, and not after Christ.
>
> **Colossians 2:8**

Looking again at our opening scripture, Numbers 23:19, notice the second part of the verse: "hath he *said*, and shall he not *do it*? or hath he *spoken*, and shall he not *make it good*?"

When God says He is going to do something for us, such as protect us and keep us safe from harm, He makes good on His promises.

In life, even our closest friends have told us they would be there for us when we needed them. However, when the moment of truth arrived and we made our necessity known, our friends failed us.

Although their intentions are pure, people sometimes let us down. Thank God, He does not work this way. If He *says it*, He will *do it*!

A Covenant-Keeping God

An old adage reads, "A man's name is only as good as his word." How good is God's word? Psalm 138:2 says that God has multiplied the value of His Word *above* the worth of His own name!

> **...For thou hast magnified thy word above all thy name.**

God says, "My Word is not *just as good* as My name; I place My Word on a higher plane!" God is acknowledging and conveying to us that in His eyes, His Word holds greater significance and importance than *the* name, which is "higher than any other name" (Hebrews 6:13).

Throughout the Bible, God confirms to us that He does not take His words lightly, nor does He go back on His words.

> **My covenant *will I not break, nor alter the thing that is gone out of my lips.***
>
> **Psalm 89:34**

> **He hath given meat unto them that fear Him: He will ever be mindful of His covenant.**
>
> **Psalm 111:5**

> **Know therefore that the Lord thy God, he is God, the faithful God, which keepeth covenant and mercy with them that love him and keep his commandments to a thousand generations.**
>
> **Deuteronomy 7:9**

God is faithful to us. He is true to the words, promises, and vows that are part of His covenant or binding contract with His people. The court system is full of individuals and companies in turmoil with one another, because one or both parties did not honor his part of the agreement. Hollywood touts no shortage of television series that thrive on such quarrelsome disputes: neighbor against neighbor, ex-husband versus ex-wife, dog owners against cat lovers; the list is pitifully endless.

This is not the case with God. Wherever we read in God's Word that He has insured us His protection, He will respect His Word and keep His end of the deal. God was a covenant-keeper when He made these statements to His people then, and He is a covenant-keeper today! God will keep His Word "to a thousand generations."

Time has no effect on God's ability to recollect His promises to us. His Word is just as powerful and meaningful throughout all ages. Jesus told us, "Heaven and earth shall pass away: but my words shall not pass away" (Luke 21:33).

No Respecter of Persons

A final example of the endurance of God's Word is found in Isaiah 40:8.

> **The grass withereth, the flower fadeth:**
> **but *the word of our God shall stand forever.***

Many Christians do not believe that all of God's promises pertain to them. Throughout the Bible God specifically speaks to a certain individual or group of people such as Moses or the Israelites. Some people assume that whatever God said in these particular instances applies only to the specific party addressed. But notice what the apostle Luke writes in Acts10:34–35:

> **...Of a truth I perceive that *God is no respecter of persons*:**
> **But in every nation he that feareth Him, and worketh righteousness, is accepted with Him.**

God is not biased and He does not play favorites. God does not convey certain rights or privileges to one person while someone else does without them. *Every* promise that God has ever made to *any* believer is available to the rest of the Body of Christ. We can further deduce this by the following point made in Acts 10:36–48. Luke writes that salvation and spiritual gifts are available to "*all* who will believe."

In a portion of Paul's letter to the Christians in Rome, he reiterates a similar message of equality:

> **But glory, honour, and peace to *every man* that worketh good; to the Jew first, and *also* to the Gentile:**
> **For there is no respect of persons with God.**
>
> **Romans 2:10–11**

The ultimate assurance that we can partake of all the Old and New Testament promises is found in Galatians 3. Paul writes that Christians have the same blessings that Abraham and his *seed* (spiritual children) enjoyed because of Abraham's covenant with God.

> **Know ye therefore that *they which are of faith*, the same are the children of Abraham.**
> **And the scripture, foreseeing that God would justify the heathen through faith, preached before the gospel unto Abraham, saying, In thee shall *all nations* be blessed.**
> **So then *they which be of faith are blessed with faithful Abraham.***
> **...There is neither Jew nor Greek, there is neither bond nor free, there is neither male nor female: for ye are all one in Christ Jesus.**
> **And *if ye be Christ's, then are ye Abraham's seed, and heirs according to the promise.***
>
> **Galatians 3:7–9, 28–29**

In this letter to the church in Galatia, Paul writes to "they which are of faith," and to "those which be Christ's." God does not consider our religious background or our position in life and then qualify us to partake of His blessings. Trusting in Jesus' ultimate sacrifice on the cross qualifies us as the seed of Abraham! Because we are the seed of Abraham, we can partake of the same blessings or promises made to Abraham.

Blessings are defined as "special favor and benefits bestowed by God."[1] Some of the benefits God made available to Abraham and his children are found in Deuteronomy 28:1–13. Divine protection is one of the many blessings included in the promises to Abraham and his seed!

> **The Lord shall cause thine enemies that rise up against thee to be smitten before thy face: they shall come out against thee one way, and flee from before thee seven ways.**
>
> **Deuteronomy 28:7**

Of particular importance to us are other such blessings that insure our safety. One of the simplest illustrations that *all* of God's promises are for *all* of His children, is seen in the following scriptures which pertain specifically to our protection.

Moses tells the people of Israel:

> **Be strong and of a good courage, fear not, nor be afraid of them** *(your enemies)*: **for the Lord thy God, He it is that doth go with thee;** *He will not fail thee nor forsake thee.*
>
> **Deuteronomy 31:6**

Later, we find God telling Joshua that the same blessing of protection is upon him.

> **There shall not any man be able to stand against thee all the days of thy life: as I was with Moses, so shall I be with thee:** *I will not fail thee nor forsake thee.*
>
> **Joshua 1:5**

By inspiration of the Holy Spirit, David spoke the same promise to his son, Solomon.

> **All this, said David, the Lord made me understand in writing by his hand upon me, even all the works of this pattern.**
> **And David said to Solomon his son, Be strong and of good courage, and do it: fear not, nor be dismayed: for the Lord God, even my God, will be with thee;** *he will not fail thee, nor forsake thee,* **until thou hast finished all the work for the service of the house of the Lord.**
>
> **1 Chronicles 28:19–20**

These are all examples of God telling His people to be courageous and not to fear. God affirms that He will be *with them* and will *not forsake them*.

If it is inspiration and confidence you desire, read what the author of Hebrews writes to *the Church*.

> **Let your conversation be without covetousness; and be content with such things as ye have: for he hath said, *I will never leave thee, nor forsake thee*.**
>
> **So that we may boldly say, The Lord is my helper, and I will not fear what man shall do unto me.**
>
> **Hebrews 13:5–6**

How could this same message be conveyed to Christians thousands of years later if it did not apply to them? *God is no respecter of persons*. He loves all of us equally and desires for all of His children to be blessed.

I included several scripture verses because I wanted you, the reader, to realize that God has not *left nor forsaken* any of His people in the past, and He is surely not going to start with you!

Unlike people, God *does not change* (Malachi 3:6). He is the same yesterday, today and forever (Hebrews 13:8). God's written words to you in the Bible are just as meaningful as if Jesus Himself showed up in your patrol car or living room and audibly spoke them to you.

Christians may courageously and without hesitation believe that God's Word is true! God keeps His Word, and all of the promises in His Word are still available to us today!

CHAPTER 3

Psalm 9*1*1 and More

The Bible is full of words declaring God's provision for our safety, both naturally and spiritually. It is vital for us to read the Bible in its entirety, but for our purposes, we will be focusing on certain portions of Scripture that specifically guarantee our need for protection. We will pay particular attention to a psalm that may best articulate God's provision for our safety: Psalm 91.

> **He that dwelleth in the secret place of the most High shall abide under the shadow of the Almighty.**
> **I will say of the Lord, He is my refuge and my fortress: my God; in Him will I trust.**
> **Surely He shall deliver thee from the snare of the fowler, and from the noisome pestilence.**
> **He shall cover thee with His feathers, and under His wings shalt thou trust: His truth shall be thy shield and buckler.**

Thou shalt not be afraid for the terror by night; nor for the arrow that flieth by day;

Nor for the pestilence that walketh in darkness; nor for the destruction that wasteth at noonday.

A thousand shall fall at thy side, and ten thousand shall fall at thy right hand; but it shall not come nigh thee.

Only with thine eyes shalt thou behold and see the reward of the wicked.

Because thou hast made the Lord, which is my refuge, even the most High, thy habitation;

There shall no evil befall thee, neither shall any plague come nigh thy dwelling.

For He shall give His angels charge over thee, to keep thee in all thy ways.

They shall bear thee up in their hands, lest thou dash thy foot against a stone.

Thou shalt tread upon the lion and adder: the young lion and the dragon shalt thou trample under feet.

Because he hath set his love upon me, therefore will I deliver him: I will set him on high, because he hath known my name.

He shall call upon me and I will answer him: I will be with him in trouble; I will deliver him, and honor him.

With long life will I satisfy him, and shew him my salvation.

Psalm 91:1–16

Christians who are familiar with scriptures that entail God's divine protection call Psalm 91 their "insurance policy." I like to add another "1" to the end and refer to it as the 9*1*1 Psalm, because Psalm 91 covers every emergency we will ever face and guarantees our salvation from each one. It is almost as if God customized the verses in Psalm 91 specifically for His children in law enforcement.

The third verse of Psalm 91 begins by telling us that "surely"—with confidence, undoubtedly, certainly[1]—"God shall deliver *you* from the snare of the fowler." A *fowler* is a bird catcher that uses a variety of snares or traps to ambush and confine the birds upon which he preys.[2] The Bible refers to the devil as one who sets up snares—as a fowler does—to catch and to kill.

> **... Lest he fall into reproach and *the snare of the devil.***
>
> **1 Timothy 3:7**

> **And that they may recover themselves out of *the snare of the devil....***
>
> **2 Timothy 2:26**

We, as humans, would not need deliverance from a bird catcher, so we can conclude that Psalm 91:3 is referring to Satan as the fowler. His goal is to catch, kill, and destroy humanity. "The thief cometh not but for to steal, and to kill, and to destroy..." (John 10:10).

Our Deliverer

One of the first things God expresses to us in Psalm 91 is that *He* shall deliver us from the devil. The devil and his cohorts spend every moment plotting traps that will steal from or kill mankind. Any such deadly or harmful snare that the devil might have for us has been rendered useless and ineffective. Matthew 16:18 boldly affirms, "…upon this rock I will build my church; and the gates of hell shall not prevail against it."

Even the very walls and castle-like towers of hell cannot and will not dominate or overcome us! If Satan personally built a trap out of these same gates of hell with the intent to kill us, he could not succeed.

We have wasted far too much precious time giving the devil undeserving respect. We have been fearing him instead of focusing on scriptures that reveal what a weakling the devil really is in comparison to a Christian.

> **…And this is that spirit of antichrist, whereof ye have heard that it should come; and even now is in the world.**
> **Ye are of God, little children, and have overcome them: because *greater is he that is in you, than he that is in the world.***
>
> **1 John 4:3–4**

The apostle John exhorts Christians that through Jesus, we have defeated, overwhelmed, conquered and prevailed over Satan and his evil spirits. Christians have overcome Satan!

We have the Greater One living inside of us, and "He *(the Holy Spirit)* that is in us, is greater than he *(the devil)* that is in the world." The same Spirit that kicked Satan and his entire army out of heaven lives in you and me. The same Holy Spirit that indwelt and raised Jesus from the dead is in us!

> **Know ye not that ye are the temple of God, and that the Spirit of God dwelleth in you?**
>
> **1 Corinthians 3:16**

> **But if the Spirit of him that raised up Jesus from the dead dwell in you, he that raised up Christ from the dead shall also quicken your mortal bodies by his Spirit that dwelleth in you.**
>
> **Romans 8:11**

The Scriptures refer to Satan as "the god of this world" (2 Corinthians 4:4). We understand that Satan has the power to steal, kill, and destroy those in this world; however, we also know that we, as Christians, are not *of* this world. Jesus said, "I have given them *(us)* thy word; and the world hath hated them, because they are not of the world, even as I am not of the world" (John 17:14).

We are *in* this world, but we are not *of* it. Jesus has delivered us from Satan's dominion and power.

> **Who gave himself for our sins, that He might *deliver us from this present evil world,* according to the will of God and our Father.**
>
> **Galatians 1:4**

> **I pray not that thou shouldest take them out of the world, but that thou shouldest *deliver them from the evil.***
>
> **John 17:15**

> **Who hath *delivered us from the power of darkness*, and hath translated us into the kingdom of His dear Son.**
>
> **Colossians 1:13**

We are not waiting to be delivered from the devil "some day" or when we get to heaven. According to the Scriptures, we *have been*—past tense—delivered "from this present evil world!"

AN OPEN SHOW

Jesus came to earth to cleanse us from our sins and to give us eternal life. He also came to deliver us out of Satan's hands. In John 17, Jesus prayed specifically that Christians would not be prematurely taken or removed from the world. God's will for us is to remain in *His* world while being delivered from the evil of *this* world. Jesus is able to ask this of God because of what He secured after His sacrifice on the cross. He went to hell and devastated Satan and his cohorts. "...That through death He *(Jesus)* might destroy him that had the power of death, that is, the devil" (Hebrews 2:14).

The devil is a defeated foe! Jesus got a hold of public enemy number one, the *world's* most wanted criminal, and violated his constitutional rights by pounding him ruthlessly. Jesus then bound Satan with waist-cuffs and leg shackles and mocked him by placing him on display in front of all his friends. Paul and Luke make this analogy in writing to the Church:

> And having *spoiled (plundered, pillaged, robbed)* principalities and powers, *he made a shew of them openly*, triumphing over them in it.
>
> **Colossians 2:15**

When a strong man armed *(Satan)*
keepeth his palace, his goods are in peace:
    But when a stronger than he *(Jesus)* **shall**
come upon him, he taketh from him all his
armour wherein he trusted, and divideth his
spoils.

Luke 11:21–22

If someone boxed with a prize fighter for twelve rounds, beat him to the point of losing consciousness, and tied him up with a rope, would you have any doubt as to whether or not you could finish him off?

That is just how powerless Satan truly is against us. That is why Satan has to use traps, such as our ignorance of God's Word, to get us to defeat ourselves. *The stronger man*—Jesus Christ—has reduced the devil to nothing.

I like what the prophet Isaiah has to say about this truth. He describes how surprised many will be when we finally see Satan.

They that see thee shall narrowly look
upon thee and consider thee, saying *is this*
the man **that made the earth to tremble, that**
did shake kingdoms;
    That made the world as a wilderness, and
destroyed the cities thereof; that opened not
the house of his prisoners?

Isaiah 14:16–17

To look at something narrowly means to take a good, close look. We will have to get close to Satan just to see him! We will see him as the frail, pitiful, full-of-fear little being that he truly is, and we will ask, "Is this the one?...You can't be serious!...Where's the rest of him?"

At times I think of all the criminals I have arrested and dealt with over my twelve-year career as a police officer—men who have committed violent crimes such as robbery, rape, and even murder. Their victims were probably terrorized by how these men appeared and carried themselves on the street and in their own homes—in their *world*. Yet, once they were *bound* and in custody, these same "tough guys" proved to be nothing more than heartless cowards. I cannot recall a single offender worthy of my respect or fear of him. If only the victims could have seen their attackers handcuffed and crying in a jail cell. Most likely, they would not have allowed themselves to be victimized, because they would have known their offender's true nature.

I am not going to wait until I see Satan to live as if he is a defeated foe, and neither should you! I choose to believe God's Word *now*! I believe God protects me from any deadly snares or traps of the enemy that have been laid for me. I choose to believe that God, the Greater One, is in me and He delivers me.

Deliverance From the
Noisome Pestilence

The second guarantee God gives us in Psalm 91
is deliverance from the noisome pestilence. Anything
that is *noisome* is "offensive to the point of disgust."[3]
Pestilence is "an epidemic disease or anything considered harmful and evil."[4]

What offensive, evil, deadly and infectious diseases
face us on the job? The HIV and Hepatitis viruses are
the two most common forms of pestilence police
officers and emergency response workers face. Our
departments provide face shields, gloves and solvents
for our physical protection; now we have foolproof
assurance from God that such diseases will not harm
us! God says that He has the only known vaccine that
provides immunization from every communicable
pestilence. Any such germ will instantly neutralize and
die upon contact with our flesh.

Years ago, I was dispatched to investigate the
complaint of a man trespassing and possibly dealing
drugs on the property of a local gas station. When I
arrived at the scene, I located the subject matching the
description I was given and told him he had to leave
the premises. I remember hoping that he would simply
comply with my request and not force me to arrest him. It
was not that this subject's stature was overly impressive

or that he appeared particularly dangerous, I just didn't want to touch him. I knew the subject was a heroin addict: he had numerous open sores along his face and arms. He was noticeably thin and appeared to be suffering from symptoms associated with the final stages of AIDS.

Not only did the man refuse to leave, he decided to physically resist my attempt to arrest him. During the ensuing scuffle, I received several scratches along my arms. The teeth of my handcuffs also cut my left hand. Although my cuts were not deep enough to produce severe bleeding, a large portion of my hands and arms were covered with blood. It was the subject's blood. His sores were bleeding profusely and his blood had stained me considerably.

I rushed to wash the affected areas inside the gas station's restroom. Because I knew that God guarantees protection from pestilence, I rested on His promise. I trusted that even if one single HIV molecule had made contact with my blood, the disease would be neutralized.

After several months, I learned through my sources on the street that the subject had indeed died as a result of AIDS. I have donated blood on several occasions since the confrontation, and have incidentally been checked for any blood-borne diseases. Needless to say, I have a perfect bill of health. Praise God for his deliverance from the noisome pestilence!

Psalm 91:3 also includes protection over something we all do daily. We pray over every meal, asking
God to bless our food. We do this with complete
assurance that if there are any germs or bacteria in
the food, they will be rendered harmless against us.
We know that our prayer also defuses any disease-
causing pesticides or chemicals in our food.

Don't sell God's power and abilities short. God has
told us that we are delivered from all pestilences. One
germ is not more difficult to defeat than another.
Trust that God will protect you against everything
from inadvertent ingestion of a stomach virus to
accidental exposure to HIV. "For with God nothing
shall be impossible" (Luke 1:37).

UNDER HIS WINGS

**He shall cover thee with His feathers, and
under His wings shalt thou trust....**
Psalm 91:4

The Bible makes numerous references to the
eagle, a creature symbolizing great strength. An eagle
finds the tallest, strongest tree atop the highest mountain
cliffs, and there chooses a site to make its nest. No
predator or natural enemy can climb past these obstacles
and harm the eagle's young. Still, the eagle takes no

chances. He *covers* the chicks with his *wings* while the mate is away from the nest.

Read Psalm 91:4, and visualize the heavenly Father stretching forth His spiritual wings around us. Ruffled under His "feathers," we are kept safe from all of the dangers of our environment. Anyone or anything that intends to harm us must first deal with God's "talons"— His wrath!

Moses painted a similar image of God's delivering power.

> **As an eagle stirreth up her nest, fluttereth over her young, spreadeth abroad her wings, taketh them, beareth them on her wings: So the Lord alone did lead him....**
>
> **Deuteronomy 32:11–12**

OUR SHIELD AND BUCKLER

> **...His truth shall be thy shield and buckler.**
>
> **Psalm 91:4**

God's entire, indisputable Word is our protection. We cannot trust merely in natural means of protection, such as body armor or riot gear as our defense, His *truth* shall be our shield and buckler.

I have met officers that weigh their utility belts down with every weapon and gadget known to law enforcement. Some even stockpile enough firearms in their homes and vehicles to properly equip a small army. These kinds of man-made shields, or "safety nets" are penetrable, and do not protect us from every type of weapon. Even a SWAT team member wearing his complete, forced-entry ensemble is vulnerable to serious injury and death without the power of God on his side. God warns us not to place our confidence solely in such means of defense. Instead, He desires that we trust Him as our shield of protection.

> **There is no king saved by the multitude of an host** *(army)*: **a mighty man is not delivered by much strength.**
> **An horse is a vain thing for safety: neither shall he deliver any by his great strength.**
> **Behold, the eye of the Lord is upon them that fear Him, upon them that hope in His mercy;**
> **To deliver their soul from death, and to keep them alive in famine.**
> **Our soul waiteth for the Lord:** *he is our help and our shield.*
>
> **Psalm 33:16–20**

> *Through thee* **we will push down our enemies...**
> **For I will not trust in my bow, neither shall my sword save me.**
> **But** *thou hast saved us from our enemies*, **and hast put them to shame that hated us.**
>
> **Psalm 44:5–7**

We learned that a buckler is a small shield strapped to the arm of a soldier or gladiator. Why, then, does the psalmist seem to repeat himself in Psalm 91:4 by calling God our "shield *and* buckler?" While both words mean essentially the same thing, I believe the Lord wants to give us excessive protection, the kind that only He can provide—cover from *all* sides.

Try to visualize how God covers us. A shield is held in one hand, normally the left, and is large enough to protect its bearer from one angle of attack. Because the other hand must carry a sword or other weapon, this leaves the opposite side of the body vulnerable. When a warrior's buckler is strapped to the upper arm of his sword hand, he is ultimately shielded from attack on both sides of his body. It's like wearing one big, armored vest that covers him from head to toe! Once I got this revelation, it served as further confirmation that I had been given a preciously fitting title for this book.

No Fear

Thou shall not be afraid for the terror by night; nor for the arrow that flieth by day;

Nor for the pestilence that walketh in darkness; nor for the destruction that wasteth at noonday.

Psalm 91:5–6

God knows cops work twenty-four hours a day, seven days a week. The police never go on strike and our services are never on holiday. When someone dials 9-1-1, he or she is guaranteed a response around the clock. Judging by verses five and six, God has the same schedule. Thankfully, He provides a more immediate response time and much better service. Our heavenly Father tells us that we should not be afraid of "the terror by *night,* nor for the arrow that flieth by *day*, nor for the destruction that wasteth at *noonday*."

Law enforcement officers face hundreds of situations throughout our careers that are inherently considered terrifying. No matter how many years of experience an officer has, calls come that are uniquely bizarre and chaotic. We are handed circumstances that require us to make split-second, life and death decisions. Regardless of how controlled we think we are, or how calmly we try to react, we always experience some degree of fear. "Big, tough" cops like to use other words such as stress or tension, but the truth is, these are just psychological terms for variations of the same emotion—fear! If a scene is bad enough, we might even feel terror.

God assures us we will not be afraid or in terror during such instances. Even if everyone around us is panicking, we will be as cool and calm as we would be on a Sunday drive. God has given us His Word on this on more than one occasion.

> The Lord is my light and my salvation;
> *whom shall I fear?* the Lord is the strength
> of my life; *of whom shall I be afraid?*
>
> Psalm 27:1

> I sought the Lord, and He heard me, and
> *delivered me from all my fears.*
>
> Psalm 34:4

> For *God hath not given us the spirit of fear*;
> but of power, and of love, and of a sound
> mind.
>
> 2 Timothy 1:7

God calls fear or terror a spirit. God did not put the spirit of fear in us; the author of this kind of negative "feeling" is Satan. When Adam and Eve initially sinned, fear was the first discouraging emotion the devil was able to place on them (Genesis 3:10).

Second Timothy tells us that God has given us a spirit of power, of love, and of a sound mind. God gave His children a spirit of *power* to overcome Satan's attempt to immobilize us with his spirit of fear.

What kinds of fears do we have the power to overcome? *All* of our fears! We are not to be afraid of anyone or anything. God does not want us to lack confidence in any area of life.

We have also been given a *sound mind.* A mind that is sound is under control and free from confusion or other emotions that might delay our reactions or hinder our decisions. A sound mind instinctively makes our body choose the correct, safe course of action for those under our command or authority and ourselves.

No Weapon

Although it is possible, it is not likely that an arrow would strike someone today. A more up-to-date version of the arrow referred to in Psalm 91:5, is a bullet. Bullets are responsible for the demise of many law enforcement officers. The same power the Lord used to protect His children through the era of the spear and the arrow will preserve us today. God does not change. He has given us His Word that no flying projectile will cause us harm. Any bullets that someone intends to fire at us will jam, misfire, fall to the ground, or altogether miss us. If we are concerned about any other weapon harming us, we can look at God's "blanket" arsenal protection policy:

> *No weapon* **that is formed against thee shall prosper....**
>
> **Isaiah 54:17**

Glory to God... *no weapon*! No stick, tire iron, vehicle, explosive, sharp or blunt object, attack dog, or any other implement or tool that is formed or used with the intent to harm us will *ever* prosper! When a weapon does not prosper, it is unable to succeed against us in any way. We are not only to survive attacks; we are to come out unscathed and unblemished!

A number of years ago, my best friend and fellow Christian officer, Ron, was involved in an exceptionally dramatic police pursuit. Another officer had located three subjects inside a vehicle who were wanted for a string of armed robberies and car-jackings. The car the subjects were in had just been stolen in one such violent robbery.

Noticing that a marked police cruiser was behind them, the subjects began to flee in their stolen vehicle. A high-speed police chase through the city's roadways followed. Ron entered the pursuit in order to assist the other officers involved.

While attempting to drive through an intersection, the driver of the stolen car completely disregarded the red traffic signal and crashed his vehicle into two other civilian cars. Normally, this would mean the end of the pursuit and the apprehension of the criminals. To the astonishment of the police officers nearby, all three subjects brazenly forced the driver of another vehicle out of his car at gunpoint and drove off with a hostage passenger in their newly acquired vehicle.

After another hair-raising police chase ensued, the subjects' vehicle eventually plowed into a fence. The officers blocked in the subjects' vehicle with their own marked units.

While Ron, along with other officers, were exiting their cars, the subject driver began ramming the nearby police cars, endangering Ron and several of the other officers on foot. The robbers began clearing a path of escape with their car.

Almost simultaneously, a barrage of gunfire erupted all around Ron, who was standing near the front of the subjects' moving vehicle. He was caught in the cross-fire of numerous pistols, a semiautomatic, military AR-15 assault rifle and even a shotgun. Ron could not drop down to the ground and risk being run over. Running through the gunfire also seemed more dangerous than remaining in his position with his now, lowered stance.

Having no opportunity to take natural cover from the hail of bullets, Ron confidently relied on these two scriptural promises from God for his safe deliverance. Although he could hear and feel the bullets flying by him, Ron would later testify that he felt no fear, only total peace.

Knowing that no weapon was going to harm him in this situation, Ron was able to calmly draw and aim his handgun, fire one, precise shot at the subject driver, and help stop his vehicle's dangerous advance.

When the smoke cleared, two of the three subjects were dead, and one of the officers had been shot. The third robber and the civilian hostage passenger had also been critically wounded. The subjects' vehicle, police cars, and surrounding buildings were riddled with bullet holes. Investigators would eventually account for at least seventy-nine fired shots.

Some of the officers later commented about Ron's "bravery and heroics" and about how "cool" he seemed. Still others believed it was just luck. Ron knew where all the credit truly belonged. He gave God all the glory, and credited his supernatural deliverance to the unfailing promises of God.

> **A thousand shall fall at thy side, and ten thousand at thy right hand; but it shall not come nigh thee.**
> **Psalm 91:7**

What won't come near us? Terror, arrows (bullets), pestilence and destruction. Look at the number of enemies God says will "fall" (drop dead or injured) around us. One thousand at our side and ten thousand at our right hand, and yet these things will not touch us.

When the fight is over, we will merely be spectators. We will watch the wicked be consumed by whatever means they tried to hurt us. Proverbs echoes this same message of our victory and the enemy's defeat.

> **For the upright shall dwell in the land, and the perfect shall remain in it.**
> **But the wicked shall be cut off from the earth, and the transgressors shall be rooted out of it.**
>
> **Proverbs 2:21–22**

> **The fear of the wicked, it shall come upon him: but the desire of the righteous shall be granted.**
> **As the whirlwind passeth, so is the wicked no more: but the righteous is an everlasting foundation.**
>
> **Proverbs 10:24–25**

> **The fear of the Lord prolongeth days: but the years of the wicked shall be shortened.**
> **The hope of the righteous shall be gladness: but the expectation of the wicked shall perish.**
> **The way of the Lord is strength to the upright: but destruction shall be to the workers of iniquity.**
> **The righteous shall never be removed: but the wicked shall not inhabit the earth.**
>
> **Proverbs 10:27–30**

No Evil

There shall no evil befall thee, neither shall any plague come nigh thy dwelling.
Psalm 91:10

No evil will come to us. This includes any injury, misfortune, harm, or disaster. One does not have to be a police officer to realize that we are living in evil times. Things that were once unthinkable are happening with more and more frequency. Who could have even imagined that someone would entertain the thought of entering a school with the sole purpose of shooting as many children as possible? Who would have believed that someone would intentionally set a bomb in a building knowing that it would kill infants and toddlers? Who, in their worst nightmare, could have dreamed of such horrific acts of hijacking airplanes and crashing into buildings causing massive death and destruction?

The devil does not only use men to carry out his evil. Earthquakes, tornadoes, fires, floods and hurricanes are some of the other couriers of Satan's evil. Regardless of the devil's M.O. (Method of Operation), God has said that none of these evil things will "befall" or "happen" to us.

> **The Lord shall preserve thee from *all evil*;
> he shall preserve thy soul.**
>
> **Psalm 121:7**

> **There shall *no evil* happen to the just: but
> the wicked shall be filled with mischief.**
>
> **Proverbs 12:21**

> **And the Lord shall deliver me from *every
> evil work*, and will preserve me unto *(until)*
> His heavenly kingdom.**
>
> **2 Timothy 4:18**

Notice the last part of Second Timothy 4:18. It says we are delivered from "every evil work" right up to the moment we get to heaven!

Psalm 91:10 says, "...neither shall any plague come near our dwelling." The term *plague* here does not refer to a type of pestilence as discussed earlier. A more accurate translation is, "any widespread affliction, calamity or evil."[5] Weapons of mass destruction such as bombs or chemical agents would fall under this category. This promise provides us with an even broader degree of protection from a countless number and variety of large-scale attacks.

We live in an era where terrorism is commonly referred to as the new battlefield. It is especially comforting to know that, not only will such things not come near us, but also that they cannot even get close to our dwelling. Where we dwell or live includes our homes, our work, where we shop, or anywhere else we conduct our daily activities.

> **For he shall give his angels charge over thee, to keep thee in all thy ways.**
> **They shall bear thee up in their hands, lest thou dash thy foot against a stone.**
>
> **Psalm 91:11–12**

Such an abundance of angelic assistance has been dispatched for our protection that I have devoted an entire chapter to the service angels provide for us. We will reserve this discussion for later.

UNDER OUR FEET

> **Thou shalt tread upon the lion and adder: the young lion and the dragon shalt thou trample under feet.**
>
> **Psalm 91:13**

Every time the psalmist, David, made reference to a "young lion" or "lions" he was referring to the wicked (Psalms 7:2, 10:9, 17:12, and 22:13). In particular, he noted that the wicked were advancing or preparing to pounce upon him "as a lion." The "adder" or serpent makes obvious reference to Satan.

We are to crush and oppress our wicked enemies and Satan under our feet. We will leave our tread or imprint all over the enemy.

God, through the psalmist, also said we will trample the young lion and dragon under our feet. Was God being repetitious? He used such words as "tread" and "trample" to paint a clear picture for us of how overwhelmingly and decisively we are to defeat our most common opponent on the street. When we *trample* something, we "tread heavily, ruthlessly to bruise, crush or destroy."[6]

> **Because he hath set his love upon me,** ***therefore will I deliver him*****: I will set him on high, because he hath known my name.**
> **He shall call upon me, and** *I will answer him***:** *I will be with him* **in trouble;** *I will deliver him***, and honour him.**
> **Psalm 91:14–15**

In these final verses of Psalm 91, God tells us that He is "with us in trouble." It is wonderful to know that God is always with us, but even more reassuring is the fact that we do not have to *stay* in trouble. God will deliver us *out of* and *from* trouble.

We can be certain that throughout our career, we will be attacked on numerous occasions and in different ways. We would not need God's security if attacks were not inevitable. His Word says we will be delivered from *all* of these assaults, every time!

> Many are the afflictions of the righteous:
> but *the Lord delivereth him out of them all.*
>
> **Psalm 34:19**

> Now thanks be unto God, which *always*
> *causeth us to triumph* in Christ.
>
> **2 Corinthians 2:14**

We could read countless versions of strategic, police survival manuals. We could attend the most extensive training courses available on street tactics and officer safety. We could even master the use of special weapons and become experts in martial arts, but not one of these sources promises us the one thing we sought when we originally placed our confidence in them: our guaranteed *deliverance* and *victory*. The only One who can give us this assurance of life and total conquest when trouble comes is the Lord Himself.

With Long Life

For He alone has promised:

> With long life will I satisfy him, and shew
> him my salvation.
>
> **Psalm 91:16**

God has given us all of these great and precious promises of abundant life and protection in His Word because He honors us (Psalm 91:15). Jesus says in John 12:26, "If any man serve me, him will my Father honour."

God highly esteems us as valuable and significant to Him. As His children, every one of us is continuously on His mind and in His thoughts; He delights in our well being.

> **When I consider thy heavens, the work of thy fingers, the moon and the stars, which thou hast ordained; what is man, that thou art mindful of him?**
>
> **Psalm 8:3**

> **Beloved, I wish above all things that thou mayest prosper and be in health, even as thy soul prospereth.**
>
> **3 John 2**

> **Ye that fear the Lord, trust in the Lord: He is their help and their shield.**
> **The Lord hath been mindful of us; He will bless the house of Israel; He will bless the house of Aaron.**
> **He will bless them that fear the Lord, both small and great.**
>
> **Psalm 115:11–13**

> **For I know the thoughts that I think toward you, saith the Lord, thoughts of peace and not of evil, to give you an expected end.**
>
> **Jeremiah 29:11**

God has done everything He can to show us in His Word that He desires and has provided for our prosperity and our peaceful, safe existence. Still, man's traditions have chosen to portray God as someone sitting up in heaven with a giant tactical baton, waiting for us to make a mistake so He can squash us! This kind of mindset contradicts everything we have been learning about God and His Word.

If you are a parent, you know how much you care for and love your own children. You know how much you desire that they be safe from any threat or harm. These are traits that make a good parent. If you feel this way about your own kids, how much more does our heavenly Father love us and desire to safeguard us?

> **If ye then, being evil, know how to give good gifts unto your children, how much more shall your Father which is in heaven give good things to them that ask Him?**
>
> **Matthew 7:11**

YOUR APPOINTED TIME

God has repeatedly shown us that He desires that we live a long life (Proverbs 4:10, 9:10–11, 3:13–16), yet some Christians have difficulty accepting this promise. Their unbelief may be based in part on a commonly misunderstood scripture in Hebrews: "And as it is appointed unto men once to die, but after this the judgment" (9:27).

The word "appointed" in this verse does not imply that we have an appointment with death at a specific time, in a certain place and by a particular cause. A familiar tale is told about a man who was afraid to fly in an airplane. He could drive a car anywhere, take a cruise on an ocean liner, and even enjoy a cross-country train ride; but riding in anything that moved above the earth simply was not a travel option for him.

One day, a friend of this fellow tried to ease his fear of flying with a bit of psychology and human reasoning. He told the man, "Look, you are not going to die unless it is *your appointed time*, so why not just take a flight and get it over with?"

The man was quick to respond, "Yes, you have a point, but what if it's the pilot's time to die?"

Although this story may sound humorous, that kind of thinking is definitely not biblical. This false assumption falls right in line with a phrase cops are probably responsible for having coined: "When it's *your time* to go, you are going to die no matter what."

This is a complete misconception and nothing could be further from the truth. After all, what kind of a heavenly Father would desire that one of His children live more than one hundred years, and pre-schedule another one to die before the age of thirty? Remember, God is no respecter of persons. To say that someone is "meant" to die on a Friday at 3:17 P.M., while stopped at a traffic signal is merely a pathetic attempt to naturally explain the spiritual issues this book and the Word of God address.

This verse of scripture in Hebrews simply means that every man is "appointed" or "predestined" to *physically* die *one time.* It may seem unnecessary for the Bible to have to point out that everyone is supposed to physically die *once*, but humans must consider more than just the natural demise of their bodies. A second death is discussed in Revelation 2:11, 20:6, 14, and 21:8. This is a spiritual death reserved for those who reject Jesus, and does not pertain to Christians.

Hebrews goes on to say that something follows this one-time physical death, "...after this the judgment." This alludes to the second, permanent death that the verses in Revelation address. Unsaved people *will* have to face this second, final death of their spirits as a result of having denied Jesus as their Lord. Praise God, we who have accepted Christ will spend our eternity in heaven *after* we have been "satisfied with long life" here on earth!

If we really want to get to know someone, we read about the person. We read his or her biography or any books he or she has written. We then gain an in-depth idea of how that person really thinks, and we have a better understanding of his or her true desires.

We have been reading excerpts from God's book. He has shown us in His Word that He is a good God whose mercy and love toward us endure forever. Through the promises in His Word, we have found that God desires us to be prosperous and healthy. His will is to bring us to an expected end, not a tragic end. All we have to do is believe for and receive, in faith, these good gifts of protection that God has assured us as His children, and we will live the long, satisfying life God has promised.

CHAPTER 4

Power-Filled Words

Years ago, I saw a movie about a bounty hunter who had captured a federally wanted fugitive. The fugitive had jumped bail because part of his plea-bargain required him to testify against a major, organized crime figure for whom he had previously worked. He had embezzled millions of dollars from this mobster, and didn't think he would live to testify against him in court.

The bounty hunter was supposed to transport the fugitive cross-country from New York to Los Angeles. In the process, he lost his financial backing from the bond agent who originally hired him, and to top things off, his wallet was stolen. The two men were stranded, hungry, and downright miserable. They ended up having to steal cars, jump trains, and even "borrow" a federal agent's credit cards.

After an incredible, death-defying misadventure, both men arrived in Los Angeles just before the trial.

They had grown close as a result of their tribulations together. The bounty hunter didn't have the heart to turn the fugitive in, so he un-cuffed his hands and set him free. The fugitive graciously thanked him, and in return removed a money-belt that he had concealed under his shirt throughout the entire ordeal. The fugitive handed the belt to the bounty hunter and walked away. Inside the belt were hundreds of one-thousand dollar bills.

The two men resemble many Christians, and the money-belt full of cash can be compared to the power of God's Word. Although the fugitive knew he had the money available and within his reach, he chose not to use it. Instead he chose to keep the money hidden. The bounty hunter on the other hand would have gladly made use of the funds, but he was not aware of their existence. Both men were unnecessarily exposed to hunger, accidents, and uncomfortably close gunfire. In the end, they managed to survive, but it sure would have been an easier journey if they had bought two, first-class plane tickets to L.A. with some of that money.

My point is this: even though we have discovered that God has made divine protection available to us, we still have to choose to partake of His provision. *We have to activate God's Word to experience His power in our life.*

ACTIVATE THE POWER

How do we activate the power of God in our life? We activate the power of God by our *faith* and our *confession* of His Word. Surprisingly, the Body of Christ knows very little about faith and confession, particularly those of us who wear a uniform and a badge. The principle of faith mixed with confession is the most fundamental formula we will find in the Bible. If we don't combine the two elements of faith and confession with the other provisions outlined in this book, we will render God's power to intercede in our life ineffective.

> **For unto us was the gospel preached, as well as unto them:** *but the word preached did not profit them, not being mixed with faith* **in them that heard it.**
>
> **Hebrews 4:2**

FAITH

"What is faith?" Someone might ask. The scriptural definition of faith is found in Hebrews 11:1: "Now faith is the substance of things hoped for, the evidence of things not seen."

Faith is the assurance we have inside that says with complete certainty, "God's Word and His abilities are real." Faith is a conviction in our spirit. Faith is not based on anything we feel, hear, or see. Essentially, faith is how much confidence we have in God and how much confidence we have to believe that what He has promised us is ours. Faith is the substance that tells us, beyond the shadow of a doubt, that the protection we need and are hoping for is already present and available in our life. God unequivocally requires this kind of trust from us as believers. For, "The just shall live by faith" (Habakkuk 2:4, Romans 1:17).

> **But without faith it is impossible to please Him: for he that cometh to God must believe that He is, and that He is a rewarder of them that diligently seek Him.**
>
> **Hebrews 11:6**

Abraham is an example of a man who pleased God with such faith, and he was rewarded for it.

> **He** *(Abraham) staggered not at the promise of God through unbelief:* **but was** *strong in faith*, **giving glory to God;**
> **And** *being fully persuaded*, **that what He had promised, He was able also to perform.**
>
> **Romans 4:20–21**

Although Abraham was nearly one hundred years old and his wife, Sarah, was physically incapable of having a child, God promised Abraham that He would give him a son and make him "a father of many nations." Long before Abraham held his promised son, Isaac, he was completely convinced that God would make good on His promise and His Word.

He "staggered not at the promise;" he was "fully persuaded" that God had the power and ability to deliver what He had said. It is this same kind of faith that causes God's blessings and promises of protection to be birthed in our own life.

THROUGH FAITH AND PATIENCE

...Through *faith* and *patience (we)* inherit the promises.

Hebrews 6:12

Some Christians think it takes being "hyper-spiritual" to attain such faith; and therefore, do not believe they could ever develop or have strong faith. But, God has already given us all the faith we will ever need to start out as a Christian.

For by grace are ye saved *through faith*; and that not of yourselves: it is the gift of God.

Ephesians 2:8

Faith is a gift from God. It took faith on our part to receive our salvation. Then, once we made Jesus the Lord of our life, God deposited a greater quantity of faith into our spirit.

> **As God hath dealt to *every man* the measure of faith.**
>
> **Romans 12:3**

> **...To them that *have obtained* like precious faith with us through the righteousness of God and our Saviour Jesus Christ.**
>
> **2 Peter 1:1**

Notice that we have been given *the* measure of faith and not *a* measure of faith. Think of it this way: we would not buy one of our children an entire candy store and hand the other child a lollipop. We would give both children an equal share of the gifts.

God works the same way. The measure of faith Abraham received is the same measure of faith Peter and the other New Testament saints received. It is the same measure of like-precious faith we have been given as believers in Christ. Our faith grows and develops as we put it to use.

How do we develop the faith to receive God's promises of divine protection and the rest of His wonderful blessings? The same way we obtained the faith for our salvation: by hearing God's Word. Salvation was always available to us and is available to anyone who willingly asks Jesus to come into his or her life.

> **For God so loved the world, that he gave His only begotten Son, that whosoever believeth in Him should not perish, but have everlasting life.**
>
> **John 3:16**

Although this message of salvation has always been God's plan for mankind, no one, including us, was automatically saved. We first had to *hear* the promise of salvation through the preaching of the Word or a personal witness. Then, faith came to believe the Gospel or Good News of salvation through Jesus Christ.

> **How then shall they call on him in whom they have not believed? and how shall they believe in him of whom they have not heard? and how shall they hear without a preacher? So then *faith cometh by hearing, and hearing by the word of God.***
>
> **Romans 10:14, 17**

Hearing and hearing God's Word is the only way to obtain, sustain, and mature in all of the things of God. Our faith builds as we accept His Word as reality in our lives. As with salvation, faith to believe for and receive God's protection comes by hearing His Word that covers such promises. We have already been reading about these assurances of divine protection and developing our faith to believe that these promises are ours. Once we believe that God has provided for our safety and desires that we walk in divine protection, then we are ready to make our confession—the second element vital to activating the power of God's promises in our life.

CONFESSION

Although most people associate the term "confession" with the admission of sin, this is only one application of the word. *Confess* also means "to openly acknowledge or declare our beliefs; to consistently say what we believe."[1]

For example, one can confess that he or she is a good police officer. One can confess he is a man or she is a woman of God. We can and must confess that God's divine protection belongs to us as Christians. As with our personal experience of the new birth, we must openly declare that God's promises of protection are ours in order to partake of such blessings. Recall that in order to be saved, we must audibly *confess* Jesus as our personal Savior. We had to *call* upon the name of the Lord and *say* we believed that Jesus is the Son of God. We also *confessed* our belief that Jesus died for our sins and that God has raised Him from the dead for our sake.

> That if thou shalt *confess with thy mouth* the Lord Jesus, and shalt believe in thine heart that God hath raised Him from the dead, thou shalt be saved.
> For with the heart man believeth unto righteousness; and *with the mouth confession is made* unto salvation.
> For whosoever shall *call* upon the name of the Lord shall be saved.
>
> Romans 10:9–10, 13

It is God's will for us to be safe and sound. We have been given faith to believe that God's divine protection is ours. To activate God's power, we simply *confess* that we accept all of His promises for protection.

> And this is the confidence *(faith)* that we have in Him, that, *if we ask anything* according to His will, He heareth us:
> And if we know that He hear us, *whatsoever we ask*, we know that we have the petitions that we desired of Him.
>
> 1 John 5:14–15

"...Anything ... whatsoever...." Anything we need from our heavenly Father is ours as long as we confidently ask. Whatever we ask for must also be in accordance with *His will*. God's will is written in His Word (Colossians 1:9–10).

Is it God's will to protect us? How many more scriptures would we need to read in addition to the ones covered in the previous chapters to believe divine protection is God's will for us? God's provision for our protection is irrefutable. His Word is our proof. All we need to do is believe, receive and confess what He has provided for us. Our faith and confession are vital keys in receiving God's divine protection.

> **Therefore I say unto you, What things soever ye desire, when ye *pray*, *believe* that ye receive them, and *ye shall have* them.**
>
> **Mark 11:24**

> **If ye abide in me, and my words abide in you, ye shall *ask* what ye will, and *it shall be done* unto you.**
>
> **John 15:7**

> **Whatsoever ye shall *ask* of the Father in my name, He may *give it* to you.**
>
> **John 15:16**

> **And all things, whatsoever ye shall *ask in prayer, believing, ye shall receive*.**
>
> **Matthew 21:22**

Again, we read words such as: *What things soever, what ye will,* and *all things. Anything* that we *pray* or *ask*—in Jesus' Name and according to God's Word, which is His will—*it shall be done.*

These scriptures help us build a firm foundation for speaking or confessing our faith. Recall the example of the fugitive's money belt. Even if the fugitive had offered the belt to the bounty hunter the first day of their journey, until the bounty hunter reached out and accepted the belt, he would not have seen one penny of that money.

The same is true with God's protection policies in His Word. God's protection is available to us, but if we do not believe and accept it by our confessions, (saying, praying and asking) we will go without its benefit. James 4:2 says, "...Ye have not because ye ask not."

I have prepared a short prayer as an example of what you could *say* if you did not believe in divine protection prior to reading these scriptures, or if you were simply unaware that God has made His protection available to you. If you *believe* that God wants you to live and not die, if you *believe* that God wants you sound, whole, and free from every type of danger that is in this world, simply make the following *confession* of *faith* and activate your protection policy!

Heavenly Father, I have read and heard in
Your Word that You have provided me with
divine protection in every area of my life
because I am Your child in Jesus Christ.
I believe that every one of Your
promises of safety is mine to partake
of and enjoy as a Christian.
I accept You as my total source
of deliverance from every
spiritual and natural attack upon me.
I trust You as my full-body, Shield and
Buckler from this moment on.
I thank You that You will never leave me
nor forsake me and that You satisfy me with
long, abundant life.
In Jesus' Name I pray. Amen.

RIGHT AND WRONG WORDS

The New Testament we read today was actually translated from the Greek language. Often, if we go back to the original Greek, we can better understand the meaning of certain words the translators used. For example, in Greek, the word *confession* means "to speak the same thing."[2] When we accept Jesus, we are born again into a new family—the family of God. As we begin our new life in Christ, we begin to think and talk differently. We learn a new language: the language of faith. We begin to confess or "speak the same thing" the Bible says. We confess that Jesus is our Savior and our Redeemer. Such a confession is in line with what God says and what we believe to be true.

It is imperative that we also keep saying the same things about our safety as God has said in His Word. Our future confessions should not contradict our initial confession of God's promises for our protection. Our daily words will either keep us under God's cover or deny Him the ability to continue to protect us. Jesus taught that, "By thy words thou shalt be justified, and by thy words thou shalt be condemned" (Matthew 12:37).

Sadly, most Christian peace officers have been doing a thorough job of making the wrong, condemning confessions for years, saying such things as:

"Bad guys never die."

"If a criminal is shot, it's only a graze; if a cop is shot, it's in the heart."

"If a cop so much as cuts his finger, he will die of shock!"

"There's a bullet out there with your name on it."

"It's not *if* you have a wreck; it's *when* and *how bad* it will be."

Some may believe statements such as these are insignificant, or that they are merely intended to be humorous. "It's 'Murphy's Law' of police work," some might say.

The fact is, these statements are significant. These are all lies of the enemy that were born in the very pit of hell. For centuries Satan has been feeding our hearts and minds with deadly doses of such one-liners, foolish lies we probably heard as rookies and eventually, unknowingly, accepted as truths. This is how insidiously the devil works.

I could have continued describing the ridiculously pessimistic comments I have heard in my career, but I didn't even like having to list these few destructive phrases. My goal is to bring to our attention that these are not harmless statements. If we truly believe that we will have what we say, then we have to stop talking this way and start making the right confessions regarding our safety and every other area of our life.

Statements such as these were inspired by fear and authored by Satan. Fear is the opposite of faith. Satan intended fear to work the same way God intends faith to work. While faith expects protective blessings to come upon us, fear is the expectation that something evil will take place. Unlike faith, which starts in our spirit, fear starts as a thought, a doubt in our mind. Once we speak the doubt, in fear that it will come to pass, we have birthed it into existence.

Not convinced? Just think of the number of times you *thought* of something negative and *spoke* it aloud. Recall how many sentences you may have started with the words, "I am afraid..." Then, when what you *feared* finally took place, you made statements such as, "I *knew* that was going to happen!" or, "I was *afraid* of that."

Do not dismiss these instances as sheer coincidence or blind fate. Do not believe for one second that saying something "petty" does not really matter. "It's the little foxes that spoil the vine" (Song of Solomon 2:15).

FAITH-FILLED VS. FEAR-FILLED

Thinking and confessing positive words based on the Word of God has nothing to do with "positive thinking," "mind over matter," or any other counterfeit philosophy. Rather, it has everything to do with the spiritual principle we have been covering: faith mixed with confession. It is the same principle that applies when we combine fear with our confession. The Bible provides us with an excellent example of this in the Book of Job.

Job's fears and confession brought about his temporary state of calamity and kept him in this state *for a season*. For centuries, religion has taught that God gave Satan permission to devastate Job's life and destroy his family. We have been taught that God intentionally stood by and watched the devil have his way with Job, when in fact, it was Job's words that got him into such great tribulation and prevented God from delivering him. Read the *one* misinterpretation of scripture that unjustly gave God the credit for Job's tragedies.

> **And the Lord said to Satan, Behold, all that he *(Job)* hath *is* in thy power; only upon himself put not forth thine hand....**
>
> **Job 1:12**

Notice in the *King James Bible* that the word "is" is italicized. The original Hebrew text denotes that Job was already under Satan's authority, and so the translators of the *King James Bible* added the word "is" in order to clarify the meaning of the verse. God was not speaking in a *permissive* tense, allowing the devil to have his way with Job; God was informing Satan, "Behold *(look at him)*, all that he has *is (already)* in your power." If God is responsible for anything, it is for saving Job's life. In the very same verse, God clearly forbade Satan from killing Job. The real question is *why* was Job already under Satan's dominion? Let's begin by looking at just one of Job's negative confessions.

> **For *the thing which I greatly feared* is come upon me, and *that which I was afraid of* is come unto me.**
>
> **I was not in safety, neither had I rest, *neither was I quiet;* yet *(consequently)*[3] trouble came.**
>
> **Job 3:24–25**

Job was doing some major league worrying *before* he began to suffer Satan's wrath. For he said, "The thing which I *greatly feared*...and *that which I was afraid of* has happened to me." Clearly, Job was confessing his fears and fretting to the extent that he was not sleeping well. He states, "Neither was I quiet...neither had I rest." Rather than place his faith in God's ability to keep his family and himself secure, Job chose to confess his fears until they "came upon him."

Throughout his ordeal, Job continued speaking in fear. Job's best-known negative confession is still misconstrued by some Christians to this day. Job 1:21 says, "...the Lord gave, and the Lord hath taken away...."

One cannot attend a funeral without hearing the minister quote this verse from Job, implying that God *took* the deceased person. Throughout the entire Bible, we will find only two instances where God actually *took* someone to be with Him: Enoch and Elijah were the only persons who, gloriously and willingly, were taken to heaven by God without experiencing a natural death (Genesis 5:24, 2 Kings 2:11).

Job was only half right: the Lord does give, but it is Satan who takes. He comes to steal, kill, and destroy if we permit him to do so either by our words or by our actions.

> **Then the Lord answered Job out of the**
> **whirlwind, and said,**
> **Who is this that darkeneth counsel by**
> *words without knowledge?*
>
> **Job 38:1–2**

God had to show up in the form of a whirlwind to get Job's attention and set him straight. God reminded Job that *He* is the creator of heaven and earth. God took the time to show Job that *He* is still the Almighty. He showed Job that *He* is bigger than Job's problems and that *He* is still in the business of answering prayers if Job will just speak rightly and not use "words without knowledge." Job's faith was rebuilt, and he repented of his wrong confessions of fear and despair.

> *I know that thou canst do everything,* **and**
> **that no thought can be withholden from thee.**
> **Who is he** *(Job)* **that hideth counsel with-**
> **out knowledge?** *Therefore have I uttered that*
> *I understood not;* **things too wonderful for**
> **me which I knew not.**
> **Hear, I beseech thee, and I will speak: I**
> **will demand of thee, and declare thou unto**
> **me.**
>
> **Job 42:2–4**

In paraphrasing, "You can do everything, Lord, including deliver me from my grim situation. You know I have said some things that I should not have said. But listen, I will make my requests known to You and proclaim You and Your blessings upon me."

Finally, Job made a good, faith-filled confession. It took a season of unthinkable calamities, but Job finally realized the value of saying the right things in faith as opposed to speaking condemning vanities in fear. Once Job stopped his crying and pitiful display of what he thought was humility, God was able to deliver him from his tribulation and give him a double portion of his original riches and blessings. God was able to act on Job's behalf only *after* Job began to speak rightly.

We don't want to be too critical of Job since most, if not all, of us have indulged in a few pity parties at one time or another. Surely, we are all guilty of saying things that are not in line with God's Word and will for us. Thank God, He provided us with a written account of Job's experiences so we could learn from his mistakes. Thank God for every scripture He has provided to teach us about the importance of our words.

THE POWER OF THE TONGUE

The New Testament Book of James helps us better understand and appreciate the potency of our speech and the creative effect it has on our physical and spiritual surroundings.

> **Behold, we put bits in the horses' mouths,
> that they may obey us; and we turn about
> their whole body.**

> Behold also the ships, which though they be so great, and are driven of fierce winds, yet are they turned about with a very small helm, whithersoever the governor listeth.
>
> Even so the tongue is a little member, and boasteth great things. Behold, how great a matter a little fire kindleth!
>
> And the tongue is a fire, a world of iniquity: so is the tongue among our members, that it defileth the whole body, and setteth on fire the course of nature; and it is set on fire of hell.
>
> For every kind of beasts, and of birds, and of serpents, and of the things in the sea, is tamed, and hath been tamed of mankind:
>
> But the tongue can no man tame; it is an unruly evil, full of deadly poison.
>
> Therewith we bless God, even the Father; and therewith curse we men, which are made after the similtude of God.
>
> Out of the same mouth proceedeth blessing and cursing.
>
> James 3:3–10

The tongue is compared to the bit in a horse's mouth and the helm or steering wheel of a great ship: two small parts in comparison to the body on which each piece belongs. Yet they, like our tongue, determine the direction and course each will take. A small bit can cause a horse to trot on a cleared, scenic path or charge swiftly off a steep cliff. A ship's captain can safely steady the helm in a direct course to its intended destination, or he can abruptly steer into a raging hurricane. Likewise, the words we speak with our tongue control our destiny.

The tongue is also likened to a small fire used to kindle a greater, untamable flame, which no man (without God) can control. With the same tongue, we bless God and curse men, who are made in God's likeness. The weathered rhyme, "Sticks and stones may break my bones but words can never hurt me," is nothing more than a bold lie. Think of how often people have been driven to angrily commit heinous crimes as a result of a few "harmless" words. Try telling a child throughout his adolescent years, "You will never amount to anything," and see if it has any bearing on the person he becomes.

With our tongue we have the ability to receive and convey God's favor and benefits, and with the same tongue we can bring misfortune and troubles upon others and ourselves.

I think of the thousands who flock to seminars and meetings when a well-known and successful speaker is giving a presentation. Many are willing to pay hundreds and even thousands of dollars for a seat. Everyone wants to hear what the "experts" in their field have to say. Although God has already provided us with some of the greatest teachers on wisdom, few of us have concerned ourselves with discovering what they had to say. King Solomon, for instance, was the

wisest, natural-born man ever to have walked the face
of the earth (1 Kings 3:12). By inspiration of the Holy
Spirit, Solomon also taught the immeasurable power
of our confession—right or wrong.

> **The wicked is snared by the transgres-
> sions of his lips: but the just shall come out
> of trouble.**
>
> **Proverbs 12:13**

> **A man's belly** *(spirit)* **shall be satisfied with
> the fruit of his mouth; and with the increase
> of his lips shall he be filled.**
>
> **Proverbs 18:20**

> **Death and life are in the power of the
> tongue.**
>
> **Proverbs 18:21**

> **Thou art snared with the words of thy
> mouth, thou art taken with the words of thy
> mouth.**
>
> **Proverbs 6:2**

> **The mouth of a righteous man is a well of
> life: but violence covereth the mouth of the
> wicked.**
>
> **Proverbs 10:11**

> **The words of the wicked are to lie in wait for blood: but the mouth of the upright shall deliver them.**
>
> **Proverbs 12:6**

God has shown us throughout the Bible that our speech is not to be considered idle. It was with words that we gained heaven, and with words that we will sustain life. Jesus specifically said that His words are "spirit, and they are life" (John 6:63). When we *speak* what we *believe*, whether positive or negative, blessing or cursing, our words are *spirit* and *alive* (Proverbs 10:11, 18:21). Our words have an immediate effect on both the spiritual and natural world. What we say can either bring us destruction or keep us divinely protected.

Do What the Father Does

God's abiding law of believing and confessing made the universe a reality. It is this "spiritual law" that is actually responsible for creating heaven and earth.

> **Through faith we understand that *the worlds were framed by the word of God,* so that things which are seen were not made of things which do appear.**
>
> **Hebrews 11:3**

> *By the word of the Lord were the heavens made*; **and all the host of them** *by the breath of his mouth.*
>
> **Psalm 33:6**

The Lord did not mold the galaxies with His hands or assemble the solar systems like a giant science project "by the sweat of His brow." Anything God *imagined* would be *good* to create for us, He merely *spoke* into existence. Recall some of the verses in the first chapter of Genesis:

> **And God** *said,* **Let there be light:** *and there was light.*
>
> **Genesis 1:3**

> **And God** *said,* **Let there be a firmament in the midst of the waters, and let it divide the waters from the waters...** *and it was so.*
>
> **Genesis 1:6–7**

> **And God** *said,* **Let the waters under the heaven be gathered together unto one place, and let the dry land appear:** *and it was so.*
>
> **Genesis 1:9**

If we continue reading Genesis, we see a pattern throughout the entire process of creation. God *confessed* His *beliefs* into *being*. Although we are not supposed to be functioning on such a large scale, we are created in God's image and are designed to operate on the earth in the same method: by believing and speaking. God's image is more than a physical image of two arms, two legs, and a head. God the Father, God the Son, and God the Holy Spirit are known as the trinity (Matthew 3:16–17). Similarly, we are triune beings. We are spirit, we have a soul—comprised of our emotions, our will, and our intellect—and we dwell in a body (1 Thessalonians 5:23). We live in the earth's *natural* arena and are part of a greater, *spirit* realm, which supercedes our physical world.

> **While we look not at the things which are seen, but at the things which are not seen: for the things which are seen are temporal; but the things which are not seen are eternal.**
> **2 Corinthians 4:18**

In the natural world of "things which are seen," we have to follow and obey certain laws, such as the law of gravity and the laws of physics. Although we have the option to disregard these natural principles, doing so would have tragic results. For example, if we intentionally jumped from the top of a tall building, we would fall to our death. Likewise, if we violate natural laws pertaining to electricity by ignoring warnings and grabbing a power line, we risk being seriously shocked. These are simple, *natural* realities.

In the spiritual kingdom of "things which are not seen," we follow the spiritual law of *speaking* things that we *believe* into existence the same way God does. We can choose to ignore this spiritual law and risk suffering far more serious consequences than if we violated the natural laws we just mentioned.

> **We having the same spirit of faith, according as it is written, I believed, and therefore have I spoken; *we also believe, and therefore speak.***
>
> **2 Corinthians 4:13**

Presentations based on positive thinking and positive speaking are so popular and appealing to our senses because the principles work. However, such information is nothing more than a cheap imitation of God's original design for us in His Word. Positive thinking originates from the soulish realm, disregarding the spirit. The living Word of God is the true source and power behind our positive faith confessions.

SAY WHAT THE FATHER SAYS

What should Christians be saying? The Bible says that we are to "imitate" or "follow" God like children do their fathers (Ephesians 5:1). We need to speak as our heavenly Father speaks, and repeat the words He

has given us to say in the Scriptures. We must confess
or say the same thing God says.

> *This book of the law shall not depart out*
> *of thy mouth;* **but thou shall meditate therein**
> **day and night, that thou mayest observe to**
> **do according to all that is written therein:**
> *for then thou shalt make thy way prosperous,*
> *and then thou shalt have good success.*
>
> **Joshua 1:8**

God is not making a suggestion to us in this verse;
He is giving us wise instruction. We should never stop
speaking God's promises and provisions for our safety.
After meditating on God's words, we are required to
add them to our daily conversations. Instead of making negative confessions such as those previously
mentioned, we say what God says is true about us. Stop
making wrong declarations that imply failure, defeat
or weakness.

> *Let no corrupt communication proceed out*
> *of your mouth,* **but that which is good to the**
> **use of edifying, that it may minister grace**
> **unto the hearers.**
>
> **Ephesians 4:29**

Just as Job showed us how not to talk, Jesus
provides us with a perfect example of how we should
be speaking.

> I have many things to say and judge of you: but He that sent me is true; and *I speak to the world those things which I have heard of him...*
>
> When ye have lifted up the Son of man, then shall ye know that I am He, and that I do nothing of myself; but *as my father hath taught me I speak these things...*
>
> ...If ye *continue in my word,* then are ye my disciples indeed;
>
> And ye shall know the truth, and the truth shall make you free.
>
> **John 8:26, 28–29, 31–32**

Confess to the world the words that you have heard the Father say to you about your safety. Let the words that *He* has taught you come out of your mouth—words that will edify or build your faith and benefit you. Speak words that will keep you in the protective *grace* of God. For example, rather than saying, "You never know when it will be your turn to go," declare, "The Lord satisfies me with *long* life according to Psalm 91:16."

Instead of confessing, "I would rather be stabbed than shot," say, "No weapon formed against me shall prosper."

Don't say, "I am afraid of domestic disturbance calls; statistically, they are the worst."

Confess, "Fear has no part in me, God has given me a spirit of power in its place."

Talk the way the Father and the Son talk. Speak boldly, victoriously and positively. Speak words of life and health with confidence! "Be a doer of the word and not a hearer only" (James 1:22).

Continue to be a doer of the Word. Talk rightly in your daily conversations. Aside from this, read Psalm 91 and other related scriptures that guarantee your protection. Apply these verses of scripture to yourself by reading them aloud and in the first person. Do as the Psalmist David instructed and, "*say* of the Lord, He is my refuge and my fortress: my God; in Him will I trust" (Psalm 91:2).

Turn your speech into *a well of life.* The following statements are faith confessions that should take the place of any corrupt communications concerning your safety.

Greater is He that is in me than he that is in the world.

(1 John 4:4)

God has not given me a spirit of fear but of power, and of love, and of a sound, disciplined mind under control.

(2 Timothy 1:7)

The Lord is my light and my salvation. The Lord is my strength and I fear nothing and no one.

(Psalm 27:1)

The Lord will never leave me nor forsake me.
I will not fear what man shall do unto me.

(Hebrews 13:5–6)

The Lord is my help and my full-body shield.
He protects me from head to toe and in my pathway is life, not death.

(Psalm 33:20, Proverbs 12:28)

The Lord delivers me from every snare of Satan and the wicked.

(Psalm 91:3)

A thousand shall fall at my side and ten thousand at my right hand, but terror and destruction cannot touch me.

(Psalm 91:5–7)

No evil shall befall me; neither shall any plague come near my dwelling.

(Psalm 91:10)

The Lord delivers me from my enemies and from my troubles. He satisfies me with long life.

(Psalm 91:14–16)

I am strong in the Lord and in the power of His might.

(Ephesians 6:10)

I can do all things through Christ who strengthens me.

(Philippians 4:13)

The Lord has redeemed me from the hand of my enemies.

(Psalm 107:2)

Hebrews 10:23 advises, "hold fast to your profession *(confession)*" of such faith-filled words. Confessing truths such as these daily will set you free and keep you "free indeed"—free from the bondage of death and destruction, free from being a fear-conscious person, and free from any peril or harm. It may take some time to make these confessions a part of your daily life. It will require a dedicated, conscious effort on your part. Begin by reading and meditating on God's Word for at least fifteen minutes a day. You will develop a greater level of faith and an appetite for more of His wisdom. As you hear and hear these truths, you feed your spirit "faith-food," and you will begin to grow. "As newborn babes, desire the sincere milk of the word, that ye may grow thereby" (1 Peter 2:2).

You don't feed your body a sandwich once a day and expect to grow healthy and strong. Nor do you develop any muscles by going to the gym for one week. Similarly, you can't read a few scriptures in the Bible and books such as this one only once. In order to grow in faith and reach your full potential as a child of God, you have to make a sincere effort to study and *feed* on God's Word. As you discover and study verses of scripture, speaking the oracles of God will eventually become as natural as taking your next breath.

CHAPTER 5

Your Perfect Weapon

My son, keep my words, and lay up my commandments with thee.

Keep my commandments, and live; and my law as the apple of thine eye. Bind them upon thy fingers, write them upon the table of thine heart.

Proverbs 7:1–3

The words we speak register in our ears and on our spirit more than anyone else's words. Therefore, *we* are the greatest source of input into our lives. Our confession of God's Word helps build our faith and engrave the Scriptures in our mind and upon our heart. The psalmist describes our tongue as "the pen of a ready writer" (Psalm 45:1). Our tongue, then, is an instrument by which we permanently write God's Word on "the table of our heart."

> **I *(God)* will put my law *(words)* in their inward parts, and write it in their hearts.**
> **Jeremiah 31:33**

During my active duty police career, I was required to qualify with my service pistol annually. I wasn't satisfied shooting my gun only once a year however, because I didn't believe that it realistically prepared me for a gunfight. I trained at private gun ranges on my own time, and practiced drawing my weapon with different "shoot, don't shoot" scenarios. Such training helped me to determine when to use deadly force safely. Reacting properly was engraved in my natural thought process and became more of an instinctive, physical reflex.

Engraving God's Word in our heart has an identical effect in the spirit realm. If we plant God's Word in our heart, we will be able to draw it out of our spirit with our speech. Then, instead of using words that condemn or ensnare us, we will speak the wisdom of God and experience deliverance.

> **For out of the abundance of the heart the mouth speaketh.**
> **Matthew 12:34**

Keep thy heart with all diligence; for out of it are the issues of life.

Proverbs 4:23

A good man out of the good treasure of his heart bringeth forth that which is good; and an evil man out of the evil treasure of his heart bringeth forth that which is evil: for out of the abundance of the heart his mouth speaketh.

Luke 6:45

Placing God's Word in our spirit is similar to loading a service weapon with the ultimate live round. Imagine a supernatural bullet that will hit its intended target dead-center every time. This projectile misses any innocent bystander and travels through every kind of armor or barrier in its path. God's Word "chambered" in our heart and fired with our lips is such a round. If we have an abundant supply of "Word-ammunition" at all times, we will not hesitate to speak the Word first.

Armed With the Sword

The vocalization of God's Word is part of the arsenal we have at our disposal. The Word of God is what we use to keep our sole opponent defeated. Every cause of danger that will ever confront us originates from and is under the direction of this one source.

> For we wrestle not against flesh and
> blood, but against principalities, against pow-
> ers, against the rulers of the darkness of this
> world, against spiritual wickedness in high
> places.
>
> Ephesians 6:12

> For though we walk in the flesh, we do
> not war after the flesh: (For the weapons of
> our warfare are not carnal, but mighty
> through God to the pulling down of strong-
> holds.)
>
> 2 Corinthians 10:3–4

Demonic forces, whether directly or indirectly, are always involved when we encounter situations that create a threat or hazard to our safety. Police tactics and carnal (natural) weapons alone will not bring us success against a spiritual opponent. That's why God has equipped Christians with a mightier weapon: "...the sword of the Spirit, which is the word of God" (Ephesians 6:17). The devil and his peons are always repelled by our confession of God's Word.

> And they *(Christians)* overcame him *(Satan)*
> by the blood of the Lamb, and *by the word of
> their testimony*.
>
> Revelation 12:11

When we *overcome* something, we don't just barely win. To *overcome* our enemy is "to surmount, overpower, conquer, overwhelm and crushingly defeat him!"[1] That's the effect God's Word has on Satan when we use it against him. The spoken Word of God is the most dominant force in the universe.

> **For the word of God is quick, and powerful, and sharper than any two-edged sword, piercing even to the dividing asunder of soul and spirit, and of the joints of the marrow, and is a discerner of the thoughts and intents of the heart.**
>
> **Hebrews 4:12**

Christians are to take the "sword of the Spirit" and do with it what Jesus did. What did Jesus do to suppress all of Satan's attacks and temptations? He *spoke* the word of God that was in His heart. Jesus did not sit down and have a conversation with the devil. That's what Adam and Eve and so many people today choose to do. They entertain the devil's thoughts and dwell on the circumstances he has presented them. When we reason with the enemy, fear and doubt set in and give the devil the authority to carry out his plan. Jesus stopped Satan in his tracks and rendered him ineffective with His *confession.*

Review Matthew 4:1–11.

Then was Jesus led up of the Spirit into the wilderness to be tempted of the devil.

And when he had fasted forty days and forty nights, he was afterward an hungered.

And when the tempter came to him, he said, If thou be the Son of God, command that these stones be made bread.

But he answered and said, It is written, Man shall not live by bread alone, but by every word that proceedeth out of the mouth of God.

Then the devil taketh him up into the holy city, and setteth him on a pinnacle of the temple,

And saith unto him, If thou be the Son of God, cast thyself down: for it is written, He shall give his angels charge concerning thee: and in their hands they shall bear thee up, lest at any time thou dash thy foot against a stone.

Jesus said unto him, It is written again, Thou shalt not tempt the Lord thy God.

Again, the devil taketh him up into an exceeding high mountain, and sheweth him all the kingdoms of the world, and the glory of them;

And saith unto him, All these things will I give thee, if thou wilt fall down and worship me.

Then *saith Jesus unto him,* Get thee hence, Satan: *for it is written,* Thou shalt worship the Lord thy God, and him only shalt thou serve.

Then the devil leaveth him, and, behold, angels came and ministered unto him.

Although we do not see a series of exclamation points at the end of each of Jesus' responses to the enemy, it is safe to say that Jesus dispensed with all formalities and was direct and stern with Satan.

In these verses in Matthew, we find that Jesus was *tempted* of the devil. *Tempt* means "to entice, lure or entrap."[2] In verse three, Satan is referred to as "the tempter." Knowing that Jesus had been without food for weeks, the devil attempted to entrap Jesus by telling Him to turn rocks into bread. "But He *(Jesus)* answered and said, 'It is written, Man shall not live by bread alone but by every word that proceedeth out of the mouth of God' " (Matthew 4:4).

Jesus knew the Scriptures. He quoted Deuteronomy 8:3, words Moses recorded by the inspiration and instruction of the Holy Spirit.

In Matthew 4:6, Satan told Jesus to jump off the top of a temple in the holy city. "The angels are supposed to catch you," the devil chided. "...For it is written He shall give his angels charge concerning thee: and in their hands they shall bear thee up, lest at any time thou dash thy foot against a stone."

The devil is familiar with Scripture. As we have seen him do with other verses, he intentionally took Psalm 91:12 out of context and tried to confuse and deceive Jesus. Similarly, when an attorney tries to use a law that does not apply to his case, Satan likes to misquote and misinterpret the Bible. This has caused many believers to make wrong decisions based on what they *thought* was biblically correct.

Unlike many Christians, Jesus knew the Scriptures because He had studied God's words and had written them upon His heart. Jesus' next confession was based on Deuteronomy 6:16. He "*said* unto him, It is written again, Thou shalt not tempt the Lord thy God" (Matthew 4:7).

Again, Satan tried to lure Jesus into surrendering His power by promising to give Jesus the kingdoms of the world. Because Adam forfeited his dominion, handing it over to Satan in the garden, Satan truly did have the authority to give Jesus the world (Luke 4:5–8, John 14:30, 2 Corinthians 4:4, Ephesians 2:2). Thank God, Jesus came to take back Satan's dominion and authority and return them to us! This time Jesus quoted what was recorded in Deuteronomy 5:7–9: "Then *saith* Jesus unto him, Get thee hence, Satan: *for it is written,* Thou shalt worship the Lord thy God, and Him only shall thou serve" (Matthew 4:10).

Although Satan made several advances, as he always does, he had no choice but to leave in defeat. The devil will tempt us with similar attacks. Either he will place a negative thought in our mind to cause fear or doubt, or he will present us with circumstances that *appear* insurmountable. Oftentimes, he attacks with a combination of these two tactics. In any case, we *overcome* him the same way Jesus did: "by the word of our testimony."

When frightening thoughts—contrary to God's Word—come, we do what Second Corinthians 10:5 instructs us to do:

> **Casting down imaginations,** *(reasonings)* **and every high thing that exalteth itself against the knowledge of God, and bringing into captivity every thought to the obedience of Christ.**

We cast down such thoughts with the same sword of the spirit: God's Word spoken by us. Do not entertain fears or give place to them by your words of agreement. That's just what Satan wants you to do. Instead, when Satan tries to tell you things such as: "You might die in a car accident at any moment," remind him that the Word of God says you "walk (and drive) in your ways safely" (Proverbs 3:23).

If the enemy plants a thought in your mind about being shot during a traffic stop, confess, "No evil shall befall me and no weapon formed against me shall prosper (Psalm 91:10, Isaiah 54:17). Such confessions cause these thoughts to die unborn, and deny Satan the ability to carry out his schemes.

Some might be thinking, *The devil doesn't talk to me; I'm not insane.*

The truth is, a person doesn't have to be crazy to hear Satan and his demons; all he or she has to be is human. The Lord knew that the enemy would try to destroy His sheep with negative thoughts; that's why He told us not to follow the voice of a stranger (John 10:4–5). God gave us His Word and told us to condemn any lying tongue that rises up against us in judgment (Isaiah 54:17). Any declaration that may *judge* or call us weak and defeated is a *lying tongue* that originated from the mouth of Satan. The devil is the father of lies (John 8:44). Don't *follow* or accept such lies; *condemn* them. It is our responsibility to *resist* the enemy's advances as Jesus demonstrated and as James 4:7 declares: "Resist the devil, and he will flee from you."

> **Be sober, be vigilant; because your adversary the devil, as a roaring lion, walketh about, seeking whom he may devour:**
> **Whom *resist steadfast in the faith*, knowing that the same afflictions are accomplished in your brethren that are in the world.**
> **1 Peter 5:8–9**

The Bible says the devil walks around "as" a roaring lion. This doesn't mean the devil has the ability to devour us as a lion would, it means that Satan puts on a similar, outward display as a roaring lion.

I once heard an expression that will help this picture of our enemy become clearer: "He is all whistle and no train." Notice also that First Peter 5:8 goes on to say that the devil is seeking "whom he *may* devour." This clearly indicates that Satan has to be given the opportunity to harm us—an opportunity that cannot arise if we *resist* his *afflictions* by remaining *steadfast in the faith.* The term *afflictions* in this verse is derived from the Greek word "pathema," which means *besiegement*: "something undergone, such as hardship or pain."[3] Our faith in God's Word and in His ability to protect us gives us the upper hand against the devil's attempts to cause us any pain and hardship.

FIGHT FEAR WITH WORDS

Another form of attack requiring our confession is an actual, physical demonstration by Satan designed to place us in fear and lure us into responding in a fearful manner.

Do you recall the set of circumstances facing Sergeant Duke? Walking into a house with an armed subject threatening to commit suicide temporarily placed him in fear. Immediately, he recognized Satan as the underlying source of his fear, and confronted him by confessing God's Word in Second Timothy 1:7, "God has not given (me) the spirit of fear; but of power, and of love, and of a sound mind."

Sergeant Duke also rendered the shotgun helpless when he confessed, "No weapon formed against (me) shall prosper" (Isaiah 54:17).

The devil responded by planting the thought in his mind to quickly grab the shotgun from the subject. Sergeant Duke knew that this was a foolish thought from Satan and did not *follow his voice*. (John 10:4–5)

As with Jesus, Satan provided several opportunities for Sergeant Duke to fail. Recall how bad things *appeared* when the subject pointed his shotgun toward Sergeant Duke and his lieutenant. Just as Jesus did, Sergeant Duke continued to use his confessions of God's Word to keep the devil defeated. Notice the tense: *keep* him defeated. To Christians, the devil is already a defeated foe. (Hebrews 2:14, Colossians 2:15)

Although not nearly as dramatic or intense, the circumstances I faced when exposed to the drug-addict's blood could have had just as deadly results. My first thought when I found myself covered with the foreign blood was, "Oh no, you've got AIDS!" I recognized the source of such a thought and refused to entertain it further or give it life by confessing my fear. Instead, I pronounced, "No evil shall befall me and no plague shall come nigh me or my dwelling. No harmful *pestilence* has any power against me and I call any vile germ in or on my body, dead!" (Psalm 91:6, 10)

I was not denying that I had been contacted with contaminated blood; that would have been a lie. But the fact that the HIV bacteria could have entered my body, had to bow to the higher source of truth of God's divine protection. The devil then tried to talk me into requesting a blood test and treatment from my department "just in case" God did not mean what He said in Psalm 91. My response to this threat: "God is not a man that He should lie!" (Numbers 23:19)

These circumstances are extreme examples of how Satan will attack; not all temptations entail life and death situations. The devil will routinely attempt to ensnare us with more subtle assaults.

GREATER IS HE

I recall having to transport a prisoner for another officer one day. From the moment I placed the subject in my police car to the time I arrived at the county jail, the man did not stop shouting obscenities. He repeatedly shared with me his displeasure with the law-enforcement community in a most colorful way. He challenged me to pull my police car over and fight "like a man." All of my attempts to calm him down with human reasoning were met with stern rebuttals. I must admit that, for a few moments, I entertained removing

his handcuffs and complying with his requests to join
him in a physical confrontation. Instead, I began confessing that the love of God has been shed abroad in
my heart unto others. (Romans 5:5)

I would be lying if I said that my desire to beat this
man senseless disappeared instantly. Realizing that I
needed to maintain my composure, I also confessed
that the peace of God, which passes all understanding,
encompassed me. (Philippians 4:7)

When I confessed the Word over myself, those feel-
ings of agitation left and I stopped contemplating the
possibility of losing my career and facing criminal
charges by giving in to Satan's suggestions and physically confronting this man. I felt total peace. The
prisoner, however, was still just as boisterous. He was
now telling me that he was going to kill me as soon as
I removed the cuffs.

When we arrived at the jail, I knew he would be
in my custody for at least another forty-five minutes
before the correction officials took him off my hands.
Walking closely enough to the man so that only he
would hear me, I whispered, "Greater is He that is in
me than He that is in the world (1 John 4:4). You are
not going to cause me to lose my temper and you are
definitely not going to lay a finger on me."

I was speaking to the devil and to the individual
he was influencing. The prisoner's eyes immediately

opened widely as his mouth simultaneously dropped. He was eventually able to stutter, "That's right... I, I...I am sorry."

Not only was he apologetic, he remained quiet and seemed ashamed that he had behaved so foolishly in my presence. He later conveyed to me that he had accepted Christ as a child, but had since strayed from the Lord. I then witnessed to him about recommitting his life to Jesus. A situation intended to be a harassing attack from Satan was overcome by my confession and turned into a victory for God!

Many of the situations we encounter can be handled with our *natural* physical and mental skills. In a select number of cases, like the ones mentioned, we will face conditions that will make things much safer and simpler if we respond with a *divine* "use of force."

If you don't have the spiritual confidence to respond to such circumstances yet, don't worry; God guarantees that His Word will not return void (Isaiah 55:11). When we speak His Word in faith, it is never without power. God will always intervene and respond when one of His children makes a confession of faith.

God also tells us in His Word that He will never allow Satan to *tempt* or attack us beyond our ability to keep him defeated.

There hath no temptation taken you but such as is common to man: but God is faithful,

> who will not suffer *(allow)* you to be tempted
> above that ye are able; but will with the
> temptation *(test)* also make a way to escape,
> that ye may be able to bear it.
>
> **1 Corinthians 10:13**

God is not the one who tempts or tests us; Satan is the tempter (Matthew 4:3). For, "Let no man say when he is tempted, I am tempted of God: for God cannot be tempted with evil, neither tempteth he any man" (James 1:13).

Do not be surprised when attacks come, for they come to all of us. But, with the attack comes the ability to overcome. God always leaves us an escape route!

As a field training officer, I did not expect new recruits to handle certain situations their first day of training. Tasks such as calls for service, high-speed police pursuits, or talking on the radio were not to be expected until trainees gained experience. I had extended them grace to protect them from making any costly or dangerous mistakes as they developed their skills.

This is the same kind of grace that has kept God's children alive while we walked in sin and/or ignorance of the truths in His Word. "It is of the Lord's mercies that we are not consumed, because his compassions fail not" (Lamentations 3:22). However, grace will eventually be exhausted if we persist in living without

God or His promises of protection (Romans 6:1, Galatians 2:21).

Take for instance the previous example of a new trainee. If the recruit left my presence and consistently refused to apply the officer safety skills he had just learned, it would only be a matter of time before he was hurt.

The only way Satan can obtain a conquest is if we *allow* him to win by succumbing to his thoughts or his temptations. If we react to attacks based on what we see, feel, and hear, then we place ourselves in the enemy's physical realm and we walk by sight instead of by faith. That is why it is necessary to keep our faith at optimum levels and make the right confessions so that we can respond spiritually—by faith and not by sight (2 Corinthians 5:7).

Just as I do, many of you go to the gun range to keep your shooting skills sharpened. If we are ever required to use our sidearm, our confidence level will be high and we will not hesitate to fire our weapon.

We should also keep practicing at our "spiritual gun range" by meditating on and hearing the Word of God through our daily confessions. We will maintain our assurance in the power of God's Word as we exercise our right to use "the word of our testimony" to thwart Satan's attacks, large or small.

God has provided us with His precious, powerful Word so that we will maintain the victory Jesus secured. We must keep His Word before our eyes, write it on the table of our heart, and keep it coming out of our mouth, because the Word of God is our perfect weapon!

CHAPTER 6

The Ultimate Authority

B y virtue of our *position* as peace officers, federal, state, and local governments have empowered us to enforce the laws that pertain to our particular jurisdiction. Whether our job designation is agent, trooper, deputy or officer, once we are sworn in, we are authorized by our department to carry out certain legal responsibilities. Our title gives us the right to use whatever resources are at our disposal to effectively perform our law enforcement duties. We function under the color and *in the name of the law*.

When we accept Jesus, we inherit the promises of God for our protection. Our title as *Christian* gives us the ability to use the Word of God to activate this protection. In addition, God empowered us to use His Word as a reactionary or defensive weapon against the enemy's snares. As believers, we have obtained the right to actively make demands on both the physical and spiritual arenas to insure our safety. We can make such demands because of *whose* we are and because of *who* we are *in Christ*. As children of God, we are empowered to operate under the authority and *in the Name of Jesus*.

The authority represented by the badge we wear on our chest is not as powerful as we believed it to be when we graduated from the police academy. We soon discovered that whether or not someone complied with the law was heavily dependant on the individual citizen's personal desires.

Take for instance the number of times most officers have had to direct traffic. The majority of drivers obey the officer's hand signals to stop and go in the direction they are being instructed to drive. However, every so often a select group of individuals refuses to comply, and simply ignores the uniforms, florescent traffic vests, road barriers, and all the loud whistling one can muster. No amount of angry shouting and jumping in place will stop the violator from going to his "pre-programmed" destination. Yelling, "Stop in the name of the law!" would be a ridiculously vain attempt to inspire the offender's cooperation. Although officers have the *authority* to order these daily commuters, they do not have the *power* to enforce their demands.

THE NAME ABOVE ALL NAMES

The Name of Jesus has a much more compliant effect on both the spiritual and natural realms.

> **Wherefore God also hath highly exalted him, and given him a name which is above every name:**
> **That *at the name of Jesus every knee should bow,* of things in heaven, and things in earth, and things under the earth;**
> **And that every tongue should confess that Jesus Christ is Lord, to the glory of God the Father.**
>
> **Philippians 2:9–11**

The Name of Jesus is *above* the name of fear!

The Name of Jesus is *above* the name of death!

The Name of Jesus is *above* the name of tragedy!

The Name of Jesus is *above anything* that would oppose us or attempt to bring about our destruction!

Everything "in heaven," "in the earth," and "under the earth" is subject to this highest form of authority that the Name of Jesus carries and represents. This includes angels, men, and demons. To resist the power of that Name is futile. For a Christian, to ignore the supremacy of the Name of Jesus and not believe on its influence would be a direct violation of His commandment (1 John 3:23). We must honor the Name of Jesus and place our trust in its potency (Matthew 12:21).

While on earth, Jesus *appointed* and authorized His disciples to use the power His Name possesses.

> **And when he had called unto him his twelve disciples, he gave them *power against unclean spirits*, to cast them out, and to heal all manner of sickness and all manner of disease.**
>
> **Matthew 10:1**

> **And he called unto him the twelve, and began to send them forth by two and two; and gave them *power over unclean spirits*.**
>
> **Mark 6:7**

> **After these things the Lord appointed other seventy also, and sent them two and two before his face into every city and place *(jurisdiction)*, whither he himself would come...**
>
> **...And the seventy returned again with joy, saying, Lord, *even the devils are subject unto us through thy name*...**
>
> **...Behold, I give unto you *power* to tread on serpents and scorpions, and over *all the power of the enemy:* and *nothing shall by any means hurt you*.**
>
> **Luke 10:1, 17, 19**

Jesus' followers trusted in His Name to subdue demonic attacks upon people. Devils had to obey their commands upon hearing the Name of Jesus. We see numerous examples of exercising authority over the devil throughout the gospels and in the Book of Acts. (Acts 5:16, 8:6–7, 16:18).

In the series of verses from the Gospel of Luke, we also find that the Name of Jesus can be employed by believers to protect them from any other means of harm the enemy might use against them. It is evident that Jesus knew there would be instances where only His Name could deliver us from *all the power of the enemy.*

As seen in the Acts of the Apostles, the power and authority to use the Name of Jesus was not dependent upon Jesus' physical presence on the earth. Before Jesus' departure to heaven, He commissioned believers to continue His powerful works and to use His Name boldly against Satan.

> **And Jesus came and spake unto them, saying, All power is given unto me in heaven and in earth.** *Go ye therefore....*
> **Matthew 28:18–19**

> **Verily, verily, I say unto you,** *he that believeth on me, the works that I do shall he do also; and greater works than these shall he do;* **because I go unto my Father.**
> **John 14:12**

> **And these signs shall follow them that believe;** *in my name shall they cast out devils;* **they shall speak with new tongues;**

**They shall take up serpents; and if they
drink any deadly thing, it shall not hurt them;
they shall lay hands on the sick and they shall
recover.**

Mark 16:17–18

The words "cast out devils" may bring scenes to
mind from movies involving demon-possession and
exorcisms. We might never encounter cases involving
such extreme, obvious demonic control; however,
that does not minimize the fact that people bound
by demonic influences must be set free. What is
important to note from this verse of scripture in Mark
16 and other verses, is our delegated authority against
devils when we use the mighty Name of Jesus.

SPIRITUAL USE OF FORCE

A common, life-saving application to remember is
this: When anything or anyone threatens our physical
well being, we know that Satan orchestrates the attack.
In the natural arena, there are instances that require us
to draw our handgun in response to such physical
threats. If a subject is armed with a knife for instance,
and he is far enough from us, we stop his advance by
pointing our gun at him while ordering him to drop
the knife. If the subject's threat turns into what
appears to be an overt attack, we do not wait to be

stabbed in order to escalate our use of force and start shooting, we just shoot. Just as we were trained, we shoot to stop. Likewise, the Name of Jesus stops an overt assault on us from being successful.

We learned in the last chapter that our fight is primarily in the spirit realm (Ephesians 6:12, 2 Corinthians 10:3–4). We also know that the Word of God, the sword of the Spirit, is to be used against the enemy's threats. If it appears the threat will become an actual physical attack, we initiate our "spiritual use of force" and go on the offensive. We apply the Name of Jesus to our confession, and our words become a command that *devils*, or the *people* and *things* being influenced by them, obey. The Name of Jesus insures that threats to our well being never even materialize. Using the Name of Jesus is like bringing a cannon to a fistfight; we cannot and will not lose.

The best way to demonstrate the power that Jesus gave us through the use of His Name is to look at real-life illustrations. A couple of years ago, a well known Christian missionary named Terry Mize visited my church and shared his testimony about how applying the Name of Jesus saved his life and kept him from being robbed in Mexico.

Terry said he was driving in his car when he saw a hitchhiker on the roadside and picked him up. His intent was to share the Gospel with the man. Shortly after the trip began, however, the man pulled out a revolver and placed it against Terry's rib cage. With the gun's hammer pulled back, the hitchhiker screamed that he was going to kill Terry. Terry's initial response was fear. He of course knew to confess that he did not have a spirit of fear, but of power, and of love, and of a sound mind (2 Timothy 1:7). The fear left instantly, but the hitchhiker and his gun were still inside Terry's car.

The man was still proclaiming his intent to kill Terry. Terry thought of slamming on the brakes and trying a few Hollywood detective moves, but those were carnal solutions with a very low probability of success. Terry knew that the Name of Jesus was foolproof. He told the man, "I have authority over you in the Name of Jesus and you cannot harm me in any way!" (Luke 10:17, 19)

The hitchhiker became angry at Terry's boldness, and responded with more threats. (Always expect the devil to respond; he is the king of bluff.)

The hitchhiker told Terry to pull over into a large cornfield and ordered him out of the vehicle. He took Terry's watch, money, and wedding band. The man then pointed his revolver between Terry's eyes with its hammer still cocked back. Terry immediately yelled at him, "I rebuke you in the Name of Jesus!"

When the hitchhiker told Terry to shut up and that he was going to kill him, Terry again replied, "I rebuke you in the Name of Jesus. You cannot kill me or hurt me!"

The man lowered his gun slightly and fired five shots at Terry, point blank! Much to the hitchhiker's incredulous surprise, all five rounds fell to the ground between Terry's feet.

After reloading, the man left Terry standing in the cornfield and was about to drive away with his car and personal possessions. Terry realized that merely surviving this ordeal was not total victory over Satan. He ordered the man, in the Name of Jesus, to return. The hitchhiker made a perfect, military-style about face and walked back to where Terry was standing.

The man asked Terry what he wanted to discuss with him as calmly as if he had an appointment with Terry at his office in the States. Terry informed him that there would be no such discussion and demanded his car keys. The robber returned the car keys and placed his gun in his belt line. Both men then entered Terry's car and drove away. Terry agreed to take the man as far as he could and witnessed to him about Jesus during the ride. Once they came to a stop, the man offered to return Terry's property back and peacefully exited the car.

If Terry had played along with his assailant in the natural realm, he almost certainly would have been killed. Anyone in law enforcement knows that when a subject orders someone to a secluded place, robbery is the least of his motives. In this case, the subject did eventually fire his gun with the obvious intent to kill Terry. However, the revolver did not *prosper* (Isaiah 54:17).

The Name of Jesus stopped another deadly attack and brought total deliverance to a member of our own congregation. A young lady named Kim headed home after one of our Wednesday night church services. She lived in an older apartment complex where the doors still had jalousie windows along the inside of the door frame.

Kim had gone to bed and was drifting off to sleep when she heard the sound of breaking glass. She dismissed the noise as someone having broken some glass in the alley. Kim continued to hear the clatter of glass breaking and realized that the sounds were coming from the area of her kitchen. She ran outside her bedroom and looked toward the kitchen. Just in front of the area where the sink is located, Kim noticed pieces of glass on the floor. Many of the jalousie windows from her door were shattered and missing. The opening was adequately large enough for a full-size man to crawl through, and moments later, one did!

The burglar stood up and began his advance toward Kim. Rather than run to her bedroom or another part of her home in vain, Kim boldly stood on the Name of Jesus. "Get out of here in the Name of Jesus!" she commanded.

The subject stopped in his tracks, paralyzed by the power of the Name. Kim repeatedly ordered the man and the demons influencing him to leave her home. The man inexplicably found himself running out of the apartment's balcony door. The subject fled in such a frantic state that he leaped from Kim's second story apartment and broke one of his legs. Uniformed officers arrived immediately and apprehended the burglar while still near the scene.

One of the officers shared with Kim that she was very "fortunate" because the subject also had an open warrant for his arrest. The outstanding charge: homicide.

There is little doubt that this man intended to do more than tour the interior of Kim's home. He might have seen a slender, attractive blonde go inside her apartment, but he never fathomed being confronted by a Christian wielding the Name of Jesus!

The devil's attempt to destroy a man and a woman of God failed miserably because of their knowledge of the Word and their boldness to use the Name of Jesus. Both Terry and Kim spoke to their assailants and to the demons that were directing their actions. By applying the Name of Jesus, they *bound* Satan's ability to harm them.

THE POWER TO BIND AND LOOSE

And I *(Jesus)* will give unto thee the keys of the kingdom of heaven: and *whatsoever thou shalt bind on earth shall be bound in heaven: and whatsoever thou shalt loose on earth shall be loosed in heaven.*
Matthew 16:19, 18:18

A more accurate translation of "heaven" in this verse would read "the heavenly realm," referring to the things in the spirit world. Jesus says we have been given the power to use our authority over anything "whatsoever" that may adversely affect us on the earth. When we do our part by binding the enemy in his strategies and operations against us here, the influencing forces are bound in the spirit or heavenly realm.[1] With the Name of Jesus we *bind*, or render ineffective, whatever Satan uses to bring calamity upon us.

Jesus gave Christians His Name because He knew we would forever need its matchless power. Jesus knew that the mention of His Name would always cause the demonic forces that come against us to tremble and *bow* to our commands. Every time Satan hears the Name of Jesus, he is reminded of his crushing defeat and eviction from heaven.

> **And the great dragon was cast out, that old serpent, called the devil, and Satan, which deceiveth the whole world:** *he was cast out into the earth, and his angels (demons) were cast out with him.*
>
>   **Revelation 12:9**

> **And the angels** *(demons)* **which kept not their first estate, but left their own habitation, he hath reserved in** *everlasting chains under darkness* **unto the judgment of the great day.**
>
>   **Jude 6**

Every time the Name of Jesus is spoken with authority, Satan also recalls the beating he and every demon received from Jesus during the three days between the crucifixion and the resurrection (Hebrews 2:14, Colossians 2:15, Luke 11:21–22). The Bible records that the mere image or presence of Jesus *tormented* demons (Matthew 5:2–7, 8:29). They frantically respond to the Name of Jesus the same way criminals scurry around nervously and flee when their lookouts yell, "The police!"

No matter what the patrolman's stature, or lack thereof, villains commonly react with erratic flight. The words, "The cops," "Five-O," or "9-1-1" in and of themselves do not have any real meaning. It is the *power* and *authority* behind what those words represent that causes such a response. The reality hits; the game is over; the cavalry has arrived and there are more "Mounties" en route!

RESERVED USE

This does not infer that the Name of Jesus is to be waved around by people as if it were some lucky charm or other object of superstition. Only we, as believers, have been given such authority and power.

Notice that in Acts 19:13–16, certain non-Christians failed to reverence the Name of Jesus and did not recognize to whom that Name had truly been given.

> **Then certain of the vagabond Jews, exorcists, took upon them to call over them which had evil spirits the name of the Lord Jesus, saying, We adjure you by Jesus whom Paul preacheth.**
>
> **And there were seven sons of one Sceva, a Jew, and chief of the priests, which did so.**
>
> **And the evil spirit answered and said, Jesus I know, and Paul I know; but who are ye?**
>
> **And the man in whom the evil spirit was leaped on them, and overcame them, and prevailed against them, so that they fled out of that house naked and wounded.**

Notice that the demon acknowledged the power of the Name of Jesus and the authority that Paul, as a Christian, had over him. The demon also apparently knew that the seven brothers had no legal right to use the Name of Jesus. It is obvious that this particular demon did not even recognize these men as anyone capable of casting him out or giving him any commands. "…Who are ye?" he asked in verse 15.

These particular Jews did not *look* like Christians to the demon. Outwardly, these men may have appeared spiritual. Perhaps they even sounded convincing to passersby. Nevertheless, that demon knew true believers were not confronting him. Judging by the severe beating he handed those seven men, the demon also took offense to their false representation.

CLOTHED WITH CHRIST

How do devils know when they are dealing with a Christian? They recognize a Christian by his or her appearance in the spirit realm. The devil not only sees a person's spirit, he also sees the Holy Spirit in him (1 John 4:4, 1 Corinthians 3:16, Romans 8:1). The devil literally sees Jesus inside of us—the same Jesus that permanently whipped him and put him in his place.

I am crucified with Christ: nevertheless I live; yet not I, but *Christ liveth in me:* and the life which I now live in the flesh I live by the faith of the Son of God, who loved me, and gave himself for me.

Galatians 2:20

For as many of you as were baptized into Christ, did *put on Christ.*

Galatians 3:27

At that day ye shall know that I *(Jesus)* am in my Father, and ye in me, and *I in you.*

John 14:20

In the natural arena, if you are dressed in a clown's costume and try to arrest a criminal, he will laugh and push you out of his way. You might even receive a beating. In such attire, you do not look like someone with the authority to subdue him. Likewise, the devil views Christians—Christ-like ones or followers of Christ— as figures who have both the *authority* and the *power* to demand his absolute obedience. Through the work of Jesus Christ, we are wearing the right spiritual attire (His Spirit), and we are excessively equipped with enough clout to back up our demands.

THE BODY OF CHRIST

Writing to the Church in Ephesus, Paul reaffirmed this same, awesome message.

> **That the God of our Lord Jesus Christ, the Father of glory, may give unto you the spirit of wisdom and revelation in the knowledge of Him:**
> **The eyes of your understanding being enlightened; that ye may know what is the hope of His calling, and what the riches of the glory of His inheritance in the saints,**
> **And what is *the exceeding greatness of his power to us-ward who believe,* according to the working of his mighty power,**
> **Which he wrought in Christ when He raised Him from the dead, and set Him at His own right hand in the heavenly places,**
> **Far above all principality, and power, and might, and dominion and every name that is named, not only in this world, but also in that which is to come:**
> **And hath put all things under His feet, and gave Him to be the head over all things to the church,**
> **Which is his body, the fullness of him that filleth all in all.**
>
> **Ephesians 1:17–23**

It is my desire, as it was Paul's, that every Christian come to the realization of the preeminence of Jesus' Name, the "exceeding greatness" of His power, and the transfer of this power "to us, who believe!"

Notice in verse 23, that the Body of Christ is called "the fullness of him." Jesus, the head of the Church, is not complete without us, the body. *We* are Christ's body here on earth. First Corinthians 6:15 confirms, "Know ye not that your bodies are the members of Christ?"

Every "principality, power, might and dominion" was placed "under His *(Jesus')* feet." As His body, everything "that is named in this world and that which is to come," is under our feet! As His body, we have and use His Name.

> **For this cause I bow my knees unto the Father of our Lord Jesus Christ,**
> ***Of whom the whole family in heaven and earth is named.***
>
> **Ephesians 3:14–15**

> **Simeon *(Peter)* hath declared how God at the first did visit the Gentiles, to take out of them *a people for his name.***
>
> **Acts 15:14**

THE FAMILY NAME

Think of a famous millionaire or the illustrious leader of a royal family. When the person's name is mentioned, we automatically envision his empire and his strength; we think of his great financial conquests and achievements. Children born into such families are automatic recipients of everything that belongs to the estate. We ponder what it would be like to walk in their shoes. We might even consider changing our name if it meant inheriting some of their riches.

When we were born again, we entered into a new spiritual family and we received our new "family name." Becoming a child of God literally made us *heirs* to the kingdom of God and everything it has to offer.

> **But as many as received Him *(Jesus)*, to them gave he *power to become the sons of God*, even to them that believe on His name.**
>
> **John 1:12**

> **The Spirit itself beareth witness with our spirit, that *we are the sons of God*:**
> **And if children, then heirs; heirs of God, and *joint-heirs with Christ.***
>
> **Romans 8:16–17**

> And *(God)* hath raised us up together, and
> made us sit together in heavenly places in
> Christ Jesus.
>
> **Ephesians 2:6**

All of these truths serve to give us a clearer picture of who we are as Christians. Most believers suffer from what could be considered an identity crisis. We do not realize who we are and what authority we have been given as joint-heirs with Christ. By receiving Jesus as our Savior, we become children of God. Suddenly, God is not some distant, unfamiliar being sitting on a throne somewhere in space. We begin to see God as our heavenly Father and He becomes a very real, loving Creator who esteems us as highly as He does His own Son. We now share Jesus' wonderful Name and occupy the same spiritual status as joint-heirs with Him.

If one of our children approached us and asked if it would be all right to use our last name as his own, we would think he had gone crazy. As part of the Body of Christ, we are just as authorized and empowered to use the Name of Jesus.

It was this same empowerment that insured the safety of agents from the Florida Department of Law Enforcement. They had discovered the clandestine location of a major gasoline theft ring. The operation involved the theft of millions of dollars worth of gas from fueling stations statewide.

The fuel was purchased in vast quantities with thousands of fraudulently obtained credit cards. It was then poured into makeshift compartments hidden in trucks, creating an untold number of traveling bombs on our state highways. The network of operatives transported the petrol to its final, covert destination, where it was stored in aboveground containers. The gas was then resold at prices well below market value.

Because of the size and volatility of such a criminal enterprise, agents knew they had to move fast. A task force was assembled in order to serve the gang's leader with an arrest warrant. Some agencies have an SRT (Special Response Team), others call it SWAT (Special Weapons and Tactics). Our SWAT team was summoned in order to assist with the FDLE's efforts. All of the intelligence gathered indicated that this was a bad situation about to get worse.

Once the storage location was uncovered, aerial surveillance revealed images of highly flammable, thousand-gallon drums surrounding the compound. Also in the immediate area of the home to be penetrated were numerous cylinders containing even more stolen fuel. Making matters worse was a confirmed report of the main subject's vow: "I will not go down without a fight."

Our SWAT commander was not moved to fear by such circumstances. Not only was he a Christian, but he had also learned some things about his authority as a believer. Before the start of each mission, he prayed "in the Name of Jesus" for the safe deliverance of his men. In this particular instance, he bound the spirit of death and rendered it useless and ineffective against himself and all who were under his command (Matthew 16:19, 18:18). He was certain *no evil would befall* him or his men.

How could our SWAT leader make such bold demands and earnestly expect results every time? He had confidence in the power of "The Family Name!"

As the lead man on the entry team knocked on the home's door and announced the presence of officers on the scene, shots rang out from inside the subject's mobile home. Two exiting bullet holes instantly appeared in the front door. None of the four officers standing on what should have been the receiving end of those rounds was hit or even scathed. Some were in position to return fire while the other members breached the door.

Once inside, officers discovered the motionless body of the man who failed to honor God's *ministers of peace* and *avengers of evil*. In the man's hand was further evidence of the delivering power so preciously vested in the Name of Jesus; the third shot he intended to fire was jammed inside his pistol. *A weapon formed against the righteous could not and would not prosper* (Isaiah 54:17).

It's no wonder Satan has tried to keep Christians from using the Name of Jesus. From the time we were commissioned to do so, the devil has tried to physically threaten and imprison believers who applied the Name (Acts 4:1–30). When that tactic failed miserably, Satan spent centuries convincing Christians that the Name of Jesus had either lost its power or that we were too unworthy to use it. We talked ourselves into believing his deceptions and surrendered precious family rights.

The resounding truth is that Jesus has not changed (Hebrews 13:8). Believing on His Name is what translated us into His kingdom! Our salvation is not only going to keep us out of hell, it has also placed us in right standing with God the Father. It has made us righteous!

MADE RIGHTEOUS

> For if by one man's *(Adam's)* offence death reigned by one; much more they which receive abundance of grace and of *the gift of righteousness* shall reign in life by one, Jesus Christ.
>
> Therefore, as by the offence of one judgment came upon all men to condemnation; even so by the righteousness of one *the free gift* came upon all men *unto justification* of life.
>
> For as by one man's disobedience many were made sinners, so by the obedience of one shall *many be made righteous.*
>
> **Romans 5:17–19**

> **But of Him are ye in Christ Jesus, who of God is made unto us wisdom, and *righteousness*, and sanctification, and redemption.**
>
> **1 Corinthians 1:30**

> **Therefore if any man be in Christ, he is a new creature: old things are passed away; behold, all things are become new.**
> **And all things are of God, who hath reconciled us to himself by Jesus Christ, and hath given to us the ministry of reconciliation;**
> **For He hath made Him to be sin for us, who knew no sin; *that we might be made the righteousness of God in him.***
>
> **2 Corinthians 5:17–18, 21**

Why is it so important for us to be spiritually and mentally conscious of our righteousness through Christ? A revelation of our righteousness—our position in Him—is the key to recognizing that we are no longer defeated human beings, living under the curse brought upon us by Adam's sin. We have been redeemed (bought back and freed) from this curse by Jesus (Galatians 3:13). We have been redeemed from a curse that brought death and destruction at the hand of our enemies (Deuteronomy 28:25–26). Jesus' work on the cross *reconciled* us to God and made us righteous. As the righteous in Christ, we are to reign in this present life. We reign over our enemies because they recognize and fear our family name. As a righteous people, Christians have the right, the power, and the authority to use the Name of Jesus as a source of strength and deliverance.

> **The Name of the Lord is a strong tower:**
> **the *righteous* runneth into it, and is safe.**
>
> **Proverbs 18:10**

"Chamber" in your heart the following faith confessions about the power of the Name of Jesus and your authority to use it. Add these confessions to your growing supply of Word ammunition.

> **The Name of Jesus is above every name in the heavens and on the earth. When fear, death, tragedy, and destruction come against me, they must all bow their knees to the Name of Jesus.**
>
> **(Philippians 2:9–11)**

> **I have been given the authority and power to command Satan, his demons, and anyone under their influence in the Name of Jesus.**
>
> **(Matthew 10:1, Mark 6:17)**

> **In the Name of Jesus, the enemy is powerless and nothing shall by any means hurt me.**
>
> **(Luke 10:17, 19)**

> **In the Name of Jesus I bind anything in the spirit and physical realms that comes against me; I render it all harmless and ineffective.**
>
> **(Matthew 18:18)**

The devil and his cohorts are afraid of me because the same Christ that torments him lives inside of me.

(Galatians 2:20, 3:27)

As a believer, I have inherited exceedingly great power over all evil principalities through Jesus Christ.

(Ephesians 1:19–21)

I can use the Name of Jesus because I am part of his precious Body and I have the same wonderful Name.

(1 Corinthians 6:15, Ephesians 3:15)

I am a child of God and a joint-heir of His kingdom with Jesus Christ. I have a legal right to partake of the protection God has given me.

(Romans 8:16–17)

As a born-again believer I am a new, righteous creature. Old things such as fear and unworthiness have passed away.

(2 Corinthians 5:17, 21)

I reign in life over my enemies. I am safe from all their attacks through the Name of Jesus, my strong tower!

(Romans 5:17, Proverbs 18:10)

CHAPTER 7

Constant Backup

I pulled out of our police station one evening at the start of the midnight shift. I was casually driving to my assigned sector, when suddenly (which is the usual course in law enforcement), I was flagged down by a group of teen-age girls. They seemed startled and said that a guy in a red convertible had just offered them money and drugs in exchange for sex. Apparently, I had just missed him.

I was told that the subject had turned into one of the government housing apartment buildings ahead of me, so I drove toward the complex and spotted a red Chrysler convertible. The driver was attempting to pull onto the street when he made eye contact with me and immediately backed up the car. Guilt and fear emanated from him.

I blocked the driveway with my police car and ordered him to step out of his vehicle. The subject nodded "no" and casually reached down as if to retrieve something from below his seat. I immediately un-holstered my pistol and stayed behind the front end of the patrol car. This was not turning out to be the usual traffic stop, so I requested backup officers.

While waiting for my fellow officers to arrive, the man repeatedly looked down and continued fidgeting with what I could only assume was a weapon. Once two more patrolmen arrived, the subject stooped down into his car again and then sat back up. He then finally complied with my order to exit his car.

Computer checks confirmed that the car was not registered and its license plate was stolen. There were also several outstanding warrants for the subject's arrest. A search of the vehicle uncovered the object the man was holding while I was dealing with him. On the floorboard, barely visible under the driver side seat, was a semiautomatic pistol. The pistol had also been reported stolen. What was most disturbing at the time was that the gun had a bullet jammed inside. It was apparent that the jam had occurred while the subject attempted to load the gun as he sat in his car. Clearly, the movements the man had been making were his failed attempts to clear the bullet that was responsible for the gun's malfunction. Had he been successful, he undoubtedly would have been able to fire the pistol.

Semiautomatic pistols, especially from reputable makers, are highly reliable. A round is unlikely to jam the way this one did while the gun is simply being loaded. Even if such a malfunction were to occur, freeing the jammed bullet is an uncomplicated, routine task. In this case, the bullet was actually removed and the pistol made ready to fire with the very first attempt officers made to clear the gun. I loaded and reloaded the pistol several times and encountered no difficulties. The gun was in excellent condition and in perfect working order.

If I had been shot that evening, most Christians would have said that God allowed it to happen or that God meant for me to "come home" early. Instead, the subject's gun jammed. Many Christians would probably dismiss this account as my having been "fortunate," saying, "It just wasn't his day to go." It is sad to consider that we have been so unjustly programmed to blame God for causing calamities. We add insult to injury by crediting luck or fate for our deliverance from harm instead of giving God the honor.

ANGELS ON ASSIGNMENT

Although I knew better than to think this way at the time of my armed encounter, I was uncertain about how God actually caused that gun to malfunction and insure my safety. I thanked God for months, even years, but gave little thought to what must have taken place in the spiritual realm in order to deliver me from disaster.

Then, while studying about God's provisions for our protection, I learned more about the role His angels play as our guardians. I have received a greater revelation from the Word that God has literally assigned angels to us in order to insure our safety.

> **But to which of the angels said he** *(God)* **at any time, Sit on my right hand, until I make thine enemies thy footstool?**
> **Are they** *(angels)* **not all ministering spirits, sent forth to minister for them who shall be heirs of salvation?**
>
> **Hebrews 1:13–14**

The Scriptures call angels "ministering spirits." Angels *minister* or "provide service" to us as Christians or "heirs of salvation." One of the key services angels provide us with is indeed protection; a function that is clearly indicated in the verses immediately following Hebrews 1:13–14.

> **Therefore we ought to give the more earnest heed to the things which we have heard, lest at any time we should let them slip.**
> **For if the word spoken by angels was stedfast, and every transgression and disobedience received a just recompence of reward;**
> *How shall we escape, if we neglect so great salvation;* **which at the first began to be spoken by the Lord, and was confirmed unto us by them that heard it.**
>
> **Hebrews 2:1–3**

The word "salvation" in verse 3, does not refer to being born-again. The Greek word "soteria" was translated *salvation* in this context, and means "deliverance and preservation from danger."[1] If we read both series of scriptures from Hebrews in their entirety, we see that angels are undeniably assigned to provide us with deliverance and preservation from danger.

"If we neglect so great salvation," by ignoring or denying the role angels have in our lives, "how shall we escape?" How shall we escape the hazards brought upon us while we are in this world? We shall escape by "giving the more earnest heed to the things which we have heard." We shall escape by learning about the precious ministry of angels toward us as sons and daughters of God, and by realizing that our heavenly Father loves us so much that He has actually given us constant, supernatural backup.

> **For he shall give his angels charge over thee, to keep thee in all thy ways.**
> **They shall bear thee up in their hands, lest thou dash thy foot against a stone.**
>
> **Psalm 91:11–12**

> **The angel of the Lord encampeth round about them that fear him, and delivereth them.**
>
> **Psalm 34:7**

DIVINE DELIVERANCE

A very close, Christian friend, whom I will refer to as T. J., was riding his motorcycle one morning when a car turned left directly in front of him. As a police officer and motorcycle enthusiast, I have witnessed numerous accidents with similar circumstances involving a motorcycle and another vehicle. Such collisions usually resulted in extremely severe injuries to the bike rider.

This case, however, was unusually different. Just prior to the motorcycle striking the side of the car, T. J. was "lifted" out of his seat. Before he had an opportunity to step on his brakes or react, T. J. literally flew—as if being picked up and carried—over the car in front of him.

Witnesses told officers that he made an Olympic-style somersault in the air, over the car, and scored a perfect "10" of a dive landing. T. J.'s temporary flight was not the result of his sudden braking or the actual force of the collision: he never slowed down and was airborne *before* his motorcycle struck the car! The natural laws of physics were violated and the life of a believer was *delivered*! This equates to another obvious case involving supernatural, angelic intervention. "They *shall* bear thee up in their hands…."

Such occurrences should not be so surprising or novel to Christians. Early in our childhood, many of us can probably recall hearing the accounts of *Daniel in the Lions' Den* and *Shadrach, Meshach and Abednego in the Fiery Furnace*. Like me, most of us have accepted such Bible stories as just that, stories. But God never intended for these reports of angelic deliverance to become Christian folklore. Such accounts were recorded for our benefit and for our application. Great people of God did not receive help from angels by sheer coincidence or special favoritism. If we look closely and study the circumstances that led to the deliverance of Daniel and the three Hebrew children, we will learn how to acquire the same kind of angelic help in our own lives.

In the sixth chapter of the Book of Daniel, we read that Daniel found favor in the sight of the king and was promoted to the highest position as the king's right-hand man.

> **It pleased Darius to set over the kingdom an hundred and twenty princes, which should be over the whole kingdom;**
> **And over these three presidents; of whom** *Daniel was first*: **that the princes might give accounts unto them, and the king should have no damage.**
> **Then this Daniel was preferred above the presidents and princes, because an excellent**

> **spirit was in him;** *and the king thought to set*
> *him over the whole realm.*
>
> **Daniel 6:1–3**

Some of the other leaders became envious of
Daniel's prestigious position and eventually came up
with a plot to have him killed. These men knew that
Daniel was a devout man of God, who prayed daily, so
they talked King Darius into creating a law that no man
should pray to any god or to anyone but to the king
himself. The punishment for violating this decree was
to be thrown into a den of lions.

Look closely at Daniel's response to this set of
circumstances.

> **Now when Daniel knew that the writing**
> **was signed, he went into his house; and his**
> **windows being open in his chamber toward**
> **Jerusalem, he kneeled upon his knees three**
> **times a day, and prayed, and gave thanks**
> **before his God, as he did aforetime.**
>
> **Daniel 6:10**

Daniel was given an opportunity to respond in fear
and to stop worshipping God. Instead, he went home
and made sure everyone knew that he would remain
faithful to God and trust only in Him. Daniel opened
his windows and prayed aloud just as earnestly as
before the threat of punishment existed. Once a day
was not enough; Daniel overtly prayed and thanked

God at least three times a day. Even in the face of danger, Daniel kept making good confessions.

Daniel's faith would be further tested when the men who were scheming against him told King Darius of Daniel's prayers. Although the king greatly favored Daniel, he was reminded that the law had to be followed by everyone and could not be changed. To have made an exception would have appeared as a sign of the king's weakness. King Darius was forced to order that Daniel be cast into the den of lions.

The following day:

> ...**The king arose very early in the morning, and went in haste unto the den of lions.**
> **And when he came to the den, he cried with a lamentable voice unto Daniel: and the king spake and said to Daniel, O Daniel, servant of the living God, is thy God, whom thou servest continually, able to deliver thee from the lions?**
>
> **Daniel 6:19–20**

Daniel responded to the king:

> **My God hath *sent his angel*, and hath shut the lions' mouths, that they have not hurt me....**
>
> **Daniel 6:22**

Daniel's faith in God *and* his proper confessions during prayer were indeed able to deliver him from a horrible death. Not only was Daniel's life spared, but also "*...no manner of hurt* was found upon him" (Daniel 6:23).

I am certain that even in Daniel's day there were skeptics who dismissed his angelic deliverance as a case of "feline indigestion." How ironic that *all* of the lions were suffering from this condition. Even a sick animal is protective of his territory and can be especially irritable. This or any other attempt to mentally explain such a miracle should have been eliminated by the lions' reaction when the men who framed Daniel were later thrown into the same den. Daniel 6:24 says that before the bodies of these men and their families hit the ground, "their bones were broken in pieces." There was nothing wrong with the lions or their appetite.

Why such a distinctly opposite outcome for Daniel than that of the king's other men? It is true that Daniel was a *servant of the Lord*, but that is only part of the reason. After all, history records that many Christians were killed by lions in Rome's coliseums.

If we continue to read the Book of Daniel, we will confirm that the key to Daniel's salvation was what he said. In the tenth chapter of Daniel, we find that angels are apparently always listening to our speech.

Daniel had been fasting and praying when an angel appeared to him.

> **Then I lifted up my eyes, and looked, and behold a certain man clothed in linen, whose loins were girded with fine gold of Uphaz...**
> **Then said he unto me, Fear not, Daniel: for from the first day that thou didst set thine heart to understand, and to chasten thyself before thy God,** *thy words were heard, and I am come for thy words.*
>
> **Daniel 10:5, 12**

In the Book of Acts, we also find that a *centurion* (modern-day police officer), named Cornelius, "...gave much alms to the people and prayed to God alway" (Acts 10:1–2).

Cornelius later received an angelic visitation. Although the purpose of this particular *ministering spirit* was to convey a message to Cornelius rather than to perform a mission of protection, it is important to note what the angel said to him.

> **...***Thy prayers and thine alms* **are come up for a memorial before God.**
>
> **Acts 10:4**

The very moment Daniel and Cornelius prayed, the angels heard their words and responded to them. The prayers of these men were not just sentences developed out of their own intellect and understanding: both Daniel's and Cornelius's speech had to have been in line with God's words. They had to have been speaking words of faith aloud. You see, angel's can only come and minister to us if we place our faith in God *and* they hear us speak God's language.

> **Bless the Lord, ye his angels, that excel in strength, that do his commandments, *hearkening unto the voice of his word*.**
> **Psalm 103:20**

This scripture does not say that angels hearken *only* to the voice of God; it reveals that angels hearken "to the *voice* of His *word*."

When a Five-star General gives an order, the foot soldiers in the trenches will almost certainly never actually hear him, but the words the General originally uttered have just as much weight when his field commanders repeat them to the troops.

Like Daniel and Cornelius, we too, can and must give *voice* to God's words in order to enjoy the protection of His angels, our subordinates.

THE FOURTH MAN IN THE FIRE

It was this same principle of believing God and speaking His words that operated in the lives of

Shadrach, Meshach, and Abednego and brought an angel on their scene.

We find in the third chapter of the Book of Daniel that King Nebuchadnezzar had a golden idol constructed. The image was prominently placed in Babylon and a decree was issued that everyone was to worship it. Upon hearing the sound of certain instruments, the people were to reverently bow down wherever they stood. Anyone who did not comply would be thrown into a specially made furnace and burned alive. Shadrach, Meshach, and Abednego, as devout Jews, would of course not comply with such a law.

As with Daniel, the devil has a way of making sure such faith is challenged immediately. Some of the men reported the three Hebrew children's defiance to the king. Nebuchadnezzar in turn provided them with an ultimatum. He personally told Shadrach, Meshach, and Abednego to bow before his idol, and live, or refuse and "be cast that same hour into the midst of a burning fiery furnace." I like their response:

> **Shadrach, Meshach, and Abednego, answered and said to the king, O Nebuchadnezzar, we are not careful to answer thee in this matter.**
> **If it be so,** *our God whom we serve is able to deliver us* **from the burning fiery furnace,** *and he will deliver us out of thine hand, O king.*

**But if not, be it known unto thee, O king,
that we will not serve thy gods, nor worship
the golden image which thou hast set up.**

Daniel 3:16–18

These men could not have spoken more boldly.
They essentially told the king, "Our decision is a
'no-brainer' and not subject to discussion."

They had no fear of being thrown into the furnace
because they were confident that God would *deliver*
them. Since Nebuchadnezzar had offered clemency if
the three would compromise their beliefs, they added,
"But if not," or "Even if you don't throw us into the
fire, we still refuse to serve your gods."

The king took offense at their reply and ordered
the furnace be made seven times hotter than normal.
(As if one time hotter would not have killed them just
the same!) Nebuchadnezzar also chose the biggest,
toughest guys in his army to actually throw Shadrach,
Meshach, and Abednego into the furnace. This was yet
another attempt to strike fear in their hearts. Average-
size soldiers could have thrown Shadrach, Meshach,
and Abednego into the fire. The heat was now so
intense that just getting close to the fire killed these
mighty soldiers. Surely, no man could survive being
inside the fire itself. But the king was about to discover
what it means to have an angel *encamp around you.*

Then Nebuchadnezzar the king was
astonied *(astonished)*, and rose up in haste,
and spake, and said unto his counsellors, Did
not we cast three men bound into the midst
of the fire? They answered and said unto
the king, True, O king.

He answered and said, Lo, I see four men
loose, walking in the midst of the fire, and
they have no hurt; *and the form of the fourth
is like the Son of God...*

And the princes, governors, and captains,
and the king's counsellors being gathered
together, saw these men, upon whose bodies
the fire had no power, nor was an hair of
their head singed, neither were their coats
changed, nor the smell of fire had passed on
them.

Daniel 3:24–25, 27

The king had never seen an angel. The best
description he could come up with was that this fourth
person looked like the Son of God. Angels are often
referred to as "sons of God" (Job 38:7). In any case,
he at least had enough sense to realize that he was staring
at a supernatural being. Not only were Shadrach,
Meshach, and Abednego's lives delivered, but as in
Daniel's case, "they had *no* hurt." Verse 27 specifies
that they did not even *smell* like smoke.

I have always been bothered by cigarette smoke. I
particularly disliked police calls that required me to
go where most of the people were smoking. Any time I
stepped into a bar or nightclub for any amount of time,

I always walked out smelling as if I were a chain-smoker myself.

These men walked into a furnace, yet they showed no trace or evidence to indicate *any* exposure to the fire or even its fumes. This exemplifies the God-given ability that just one angel has to deliver us. It is no wonder the Bible refers to these beings as "his mighty angels" (2 Thessalonians 1:7); "angels, that excel in strength" (Psalm 103:20); "angels, which are greater in power and might *(than men)*" (2 Peter 2:11).

HEAVEN'S SECRET SERVICE

The president of the United States is afforded extraordinary security by the Secret Service. Anywhere he travels, our country's leader can rely on any number of agents being within earshot of his voice. As soon as even a hint of danger arises, Secret Service agents scramble into position, placing their own lives at risk in order to insure the president's safety.

Imagine if everywhere you went, an entourage of armed men surrounded you. Your confidence level would probably go up a notch or two and you would not be very concerned about your protection.

Now, consider the *reality* that you *are* always in the company of angels!

God has provided us with His own elite group of bodyguards—ministering "agents"—that are much more capable and highly trained than all of the human armies of the world combined. It was just one angel that safely led the way for Moses and the entire nation of Israel out of Egypt (Exodus 23:20–23). It only took one angel to wipe out all the guards that secured Jesus' tomb and move the mammoth boulder from its opening (Matthew 28:2–4). God sent only one angel in each of the cases we previously reviewed, and all you and I need to keep us in all our ways is one such mighty angel that "excels in strength and is greater in power and might than mere men."

Although angels have been granted such potency in their service to us, it is vital that we not speak words that *condemn* us and hinder their protective role (Matthew 12:37). In the last chapter, we learned that believers bind and loose things in the earth, and those things are bound or loosed in heaven (Matthew 16:19). As we have discovered, we *loose* God's angels in the same way we *bind* demons (fallen angels): *with our mouths.* This obviously does not mean that we are to pray to angels or to worship them. Simply aligning our confessions about our safety with the Word of God, and thanking God for angelic protection keeps angels "on the beat."

An Eternal Assignment

How can we be so certain angels are still on duty today? Were their mighty works limited only to Old Testament men and women of God? We find examples of angels ministering life-saving assistance throughout the New Testament too.

The apostle Peter was miraculously saved from execution by an angel (Acts 12:4–10). An angel delivered Paul when shipwreck and death seemed certain (Acts 27:21–25).

In addition, Jesus tells us in Matthew 18:10, "Take heed that ye despise not one of these little ones; for I say unto you, That in heaven *their angels do always behold the face of my Father* which is in heaven."

Jesus is referring to Christians as "these little ones." If we read verses three through six of Matthew 18, we find that Jesus was comparing our spiritual salvation to becoming *as little children*. Jesus continued to use phrases such as "little child" and "little ones" as he spoke to His disciples about believers and their conversions.

As children of God, Jesus reassures us that our angels are always in the presence of God, directly implying that angels are personally and permanently assigned to protect Christians! You might have to patrol some of the roughest neighborhoods in town, but with an angel as your partner, thugs don't have a chance against you!

In the early hours of the morning, during the midnight shift, a fellow officer attempted to make what is commonly referred to as a "high-risk" traffic stop. The subject driver was already wanted for a recent string of armed convenience store robberies. He had actually committed one such robbery moments earlier and was now putting some distance between himself and the scene of his crime.

Before any backup officers could arrive, and even before the officer actuated his emergency lights, the subject became aware of his imminent encounter with the police and began a high-speed flight through the city in his newly stolen car.

As any real cop would be, I was thrilled when I soon found myself as the secondary unit in the pursuit. But, as excited as I was about my backup role, I was mindful of all the factors that distinguished this particular chase from so many others. I knew, for instance, that the subject was armed and very dangerous. I knew that he had committed enough capital felonies to put him away for several life sentences. Displaying one of the most reckless driving patterns I had ever witnessed, including charging marked police cars with his own vehicle, the subject was cognizant of his predicament if caught alive. I had little doubt this pursuit would end in a gunfight.

My premonition would soon be tested as our subject made one final turn down a dead end street. As he neared a water canal's safety barricade, the subject swerved to a crashing halt. Within the same second, the primary unit and I turned sharply, hastily positioning our police cars to help shield us from possible gunfire. My patrol car stopped just behind and to the left of the subject's vehicle.

I could not have exited my cruiser any faster; I watched as the subject literally beat me to the draw. I saw him jump out of his car, look toward me, and turn around as if to better position himself for the shot. In his right hand was the grim silhouette of a small pistol. Although I was reaching for my own gun, I knew the first shot fired would not be mine. Nevertheless, I was not afraid. I figured he would just have to miss me as I moved to stoop behind my car. I, in turn, would hit my mark—center-mass—as trained.

Then, something entirely unexpected happened. Just as the man's shooting hand began its ascent to take aim at me, his wrist made what I can only describe as the strangest "twitch" I have ever seen. Although I saw no one, it was as though *someone* had slapped the subject's hand with sufficient force to cause the pistol to fall to the ground. Momentarily stunned, the subject hurriedly looked around before running off into some nearby brush.

The entire incident happened so fast I had barely enough time to unholster my weapon. Briefly confounded myself, I took off after the subject while the primary officer remained with the vehicles. With the help of our canine officers, the subject was eventually apprehended.

As I reflected on what had just taken place, I knew an angelic being had moved on my behalf. Years went by and I never shared this testimony with anyone. *Who would believe me?* I thought. Besides, the few officers who responded were convinced that the subject had "dropped" his gun next to his car. This explanation made no sense; I don't know of too many criminals who discard evidence where uniformed police officers can easily recover it.

Then one day I heard another Christian police officer give a curiously similar testimony. He said he was running after a wanted subject through a residential area, when he realized the man had a gun. The fleeing subject ignored commands to drop his weapon. The officer was obviously concerned about the safety of the citizens in the immediate area. He also wanted to keep the other officers arriving to his aid from unnecessarily encountering the same armed subject.

Having made the decision to shoot, the officer leveled his pistol toward the fleeing felon. Just as he prepared to take aim, he saw the subject's gun hand make a strange, sudden gesture. The officer confided, "It was as if someone was running at full speed in the opposite direction from the subject, and intentionally plowed into him."

His collision with the "invisible party" caused the revolver to fly out of the man's hand and onto the sidewalk. Just as in my case, the subject temporarily looked around in dismay before realizing that the police were still chasing him.

My lightning-fast mind did the math, and I came to the same conclusion my *spirit-man* had already made. Two men, whose hearts were twisted enough to consider taking the lives of two police officers, suddenly found themselves unarmed and unable to touch either *one of His little ones!*

As a word of caution, do not try to look for angels or ask God to let you see them. Comparatively speaking, there are very few recorded accounts in the Bible where people actually *saw* their assigned angels. Jesus said, "...an evil and adulterous generation seeketh after a sign..." (Matthew 12:39).

If an angel is required to reveal himself in order to save your life, he will. Trust that angels are everpresent and constantly working on your behalf, not only because the Bible tells us so, but because, like me, you can probably recollect experiences when you could have been killed or seriously injured had some

unexplainable, extraordinary circumstance not prevented your calamity.

Honor God by crediting His ministering angels
with your deliverance. Angels that "shut the mouths
of lions" also jam pistols. Angels that "encamped
around" God's children to protect them from a burning
fire still "encamp around" us and protect us from a
barrage of gun fire. Angels still "bear us up in their
hands" and set us in safe places.

How shall we escape if we neglect so great salvation?
Give the more earnest heed to what you have heard!

Read the following prayer aloud and *loose* your spiritual backup!

> **Heavenly Father, I thank You for the
> ministering spirits that You have given charge
> over me, to keep me in all my ways.
> Angels encamp around me
> and lift me up in their hands when
> I am confronted with danger.
> Lord, I thank You for Your angelic army that
> serves and protects me as an heir of salvation.
> In the Name of Jesus, I rebuke and render
> ineffective any wrong confessions I have made
> in the past in regard to my protection.
> I loose Your mighty angels in the Name of
> Jesus, and send them forth by continuously
> giving voice to the delivering power of Your
> Holy, written Word.
> I refuse to neglect the safety
> and deliverance Your angels
> provide for me.
> Father God, I give You all the praise,
> all the glory, and all the honor
> for every instance Your angelic host
> will move on my behalf
> to insure my total safety.
> In Jesus' Name I pray. Amen.**

CHAPTER 8

Scarlet Cover

The principles of *Cover and Concealment* have always played an integral role in the success of military and police operations. I was introduced to these terms early in my military career. I remember one of my roughneck training instructors telling me in the advent of a battle: "When the shooting starts, you better be behind, inside, or under something that will stop a bullet; you better be behind *cover!*"

If solid cover was not available, the next best thing was to at least hide or camouflage oneself somehow. We were to become part of the landscape and trust in *concealment*. To anyone with any common sense, finding cover was the far better choice.

Although I felt I had a good understanding of the difference between cover and concealment, I quickly learned to truly appreciate the use of cover during my first live ammunition field exercise. Classroom instruction does not quite compare to crawling around in a muddy trench in order to keep from being shot. I knew this exercise was only training, but I also realized that the bullets being fired overhead were not aware that this was just a drill. Not only was I not concerned about the filthy state in which I found myself, I was actually content to use the wet, rocky ground above and around me as cover.

Once I became a police officer, I developed an even greater understanding of and admiration for the term "cover." There was no shortage of gun-toting criminals in the neighborhoods I patrolled, and most of the law-abiding citizens actively exercised their Second Amendment right to bear arms. I encountered dozens of opportunities to seek cover behind walls, buildings, parked cars, and countless other fixed objects that I thought should stop a round. For the greater part of my police career, every time a situation that might involve gunplay arose, I depended solely on such *natural* barriers for my safety. I knew nothing of the *spiritual* protective cover that Jesus had made available to me by the shedding of His blood at Calvary.

THE BLOOD OF JESUS

As born-again Christians, we acknowledge the redemptive value of Jesus' blood. We trust in the fact that Jesus' sacrifice on the cross paid for our sins in full and purchased us back from the hands of the enemy and eternal death. By putting our faith in the blood of Jesus and its ability to make us righteous, we received salvation and secured an eternal home in heaven.

> *(We)* **Being justified freely by his grace through the redemption that is in Christ Jesus:**
> **Whom God hath set forth to be a propitiation** *(reconciliation)* **through faith in his blood....**
>
> **Romans 3:24–25**

> **...***By his own blood* **He entered in once into the holy place, having obtained eternal redemption for us.**
>
> **Hebrews 9:12**

> **...For thou wast slain, and hast redeemed us to God** *by thy blood***....**
>
> **Revelation 5:9**

The debt Jesus paid for us was so great that only the immeasurable value of His own blood could wipe out the sin deficit our spirits were once in. The shedding of blood for man's transgressions had long been a requirement from God. This was a precedent set early in the Bible (Genesis 3:21). In the Old Testament, in order for God to continue to fellowship with man, the sacrifice of a spotless lamb—a lamb without blemish—was required to pay the price and *cover* sin from the presence of God.

> **For the life of the flesh is in the blood: and I have given it to you upon the altar to make atonement for your souls....**
>
> **Leviticus 17:11**

THE BLOOD OF THE LAMB

The Bible teaches us that the blood of lambs also served as a protective barrier from danger and premature death. In the Book of Exodus, Egypt was stricken with nine plagues because of Pharaoh's disobedience to God and his resistance to set God's people free. It would take a tenth and final, terrible calamity to soften Pharaoh's calloused heart.

God warned Moses that the destroyer would pass through all of Egypt and kill the firstborn of every household. This also included every Hebrew home. Even the firstborn of their livestock would be killed (Exodus 11:4–5, 12:1–13). We also find that God provided *cover* for His people to remain unharmed. Their protection would rest in the faithful application of a lamb's blood around the front door of their homes.

Then Moses called for all the elders of
Israel, and said unto them, Draw out and
take you a lamb according to your families,
and kill the passover.

And ye shall take a bunch of hyssop, and
dip it in the blood that is in the basin, and
strike the lintel and the two side posts *with
the blood* that is in the basin; and none of
you shall go out at the door of his house until the morning.

For the Lord will pass through to smite
the Egyptians; and *when he seeth the blood*
upon the lintel, and on the two side posts,
the Lord will pass over the door, and *will
not suffer (allow) the destroyer to come in unto
your houses to smite you.*

Exodus12:21–23

An untold number of people and animals were
killed throughout Egypt in one evening. The destroyer,
however, was unable to touch the people of God who
obeyed His instructions. The key to the Israelites'
divine deliverance was not necessarily behind any
physical power in the lambs' blood; God was able to
intervene for each household only after the blood was
conspicuously applied in faithful obedience. The blood
served as a *token* of the Jews' faith and trust in God to
save them from destruction (Exodus 12:13). The
slaughtered lamb took the place of the firstborn sons
and daughters of each family.

THE SCARLET THREAD

This was not the only instance the blood was used to protect lives. In the Book of Joshua we find that a woman and her entire family were saved from peril by a similar *scarlet token* (Joshua 2:12).

Rahab was a prostitute who lived in the city of Jericho. Jericho was in a state of panic because news of the Israelites and their conquests over other great, neighboring cities had spread (Joshua 2:10–11).

Before the Israelites marched against Jericho, Joshua sent two spies ahead to view the land. The two men went into Jericho and found refuge in Rahab's house. The king of Jericho eventually received word of the spies' presence and sent troops to capture them.

When the soldiers arrived at Rahab's home, she told them that the spies had just left. The king's men left hastily in an attempt to catch up to the spies, when in reality, the two men were still hiding on the roof of Rahab's home.

In return for her help, Rahab asked the spies to spare her life and the lives of her family during the Israelite attack on Jericho. Notice their response.

> **Behold, when we come into the land, thou shalt *bind this line of scarlet thread in the window* which thou didst let us down by: and thou shalt bring thy father, and thy mother,**

and thy brethren, and all thy father's household, home unto thee.

And it shall be, that whosoever shall go out of the doors of thy house into the street, his blood shall be upon his head, and we will be guiltless: and whosoever shall be with thee in the house, his blood shall be on our head, if any hand be upon him...

And she said, According to your words, so be it. And she sent them away, and they departed: and she *bound the scarlet line in the window.*

Joshua 2:18–19, 21

There was no time to slaughter a lamb and prepare it in accordance with the instructions given to Moses and the Israelites during their exodus from Egypt. The spies were on the run and could not provide a detailed account and explanation of the Passover to Rahab. In lieu of applying blood to her doorposts, Rahab displayed a *scarlet thread* in her window. The thread symbolized a *blood line* that would keep Rahab, her family, and all of their possessions safe from harm.

This blood line was honored by Israel's invading army and, more importantly, by God Himself. It was God who instructed Joshua and his army to march around Jericho seven days. On the seventh day, the seventh time around the city, the Israelites were to give a great shout of praise. Without having to raise a sword or risk a man, the Lord caused the great wall around Jericho to collapse (Joshua 6:3–20). Not a pebble fell

on Rahab and her family. Although the noise and
confusion of the ensuing slaughter must have been
great, not a single soldier mistakenly hurt any of
the members of the only "blood-protected" residence
in Jericho.

> ...And the people shouted with a great
> shout, that the wall fell down flat, so that the
> people went up into the city, every man
> straight before him....
> And they utterly destroyed all that was
> in the city....
> But Joshua had said unto the two men that
> had spied out the country, Go into the harlot's
> house, and bring out thence the woman, and
> all that she hath, as ye sware unto her.
> And the young men that were spies went
> in, and *brought out Rahab, and her father,
> and her mother, and her brethren, and all that
> she had;* and they brought out all her kin-
> dred.
>
> **Joshua 6:20–23**

Rahab, a known harlot, put her trust in the God of
Israel (Hebrews 11:31). She acted on her faith by placing
a *symbol* of the Passover blood on her home. Rahab's
faith in her *scarlet cover* caused even her kindred—
non-immediate family—and all of their belongings to
be saved.

God's servants in the Old Testament used the blood of lambs to keep them from imminent death at the hands of the destroyer. Rahab, who was not even considered a covenant person, was spared by a *token* of the same blood of animals. Surely we, as children of the living God and joint-heirs with Christ Jesus, have been afforded at least a similar type of deliverance from danger under the New Testament! (Galatians 4:7)

Not only have we been given the same divine protection, the Scriptures reveal that we have a *better*, all-powerful source of cover through the blood of Jesus Himself. Throughout the New Testament, Jesus is referred to as our *Lamb*. His perfect blood replaced the old covenant need to continuously sacrifice lambs for our sins or for our protection.

> **The next day John seeth Jesus coming unto him, and saith, *Behold the Lamb of God,* which taketh away the sin of the world.**
>
> **John 1:29**

> **For as much as ye know that ye were not redeemed with corruptible things...**
> **But with the precious blood of Christ, *as of a lamb without blemish and without spot.***
>
> **1 Peter 1:18–19**

> **These are they which came out of great tribulation, and have washed their robes, and made them white in *the blood of the Lamb.***
>
> **Revelation 7:14**

As our present-day Lamb, the blood Jesus shed more than 2,000 years ago is actively washing our sins (1 John 1:7, Hebrews 10:14). His blood was not stored somewhere out of our reach and allowed to putrefy. When we received salvation, the actual blood of Jesus brought us to life spiritually. "And you hath he quickened *(made alive),* who were dead in trespasses and sins" (Ephesians 2:1–1, Corinthians 15:45).

Had we been able to look into the spirit realm the instant we accepted Jesus, we would have seen a spiritual "blood transfusion" from Jesus to us—a literal washing of our spirit from every sin we ever committed or mentally entertained—occurred. It is this same cleansing, life-giving blood that Jesus has given to us for our protection. Jesus is our Lamb—our delivering Passover. "...Christ our passover, is sacrificed for us" (1 Corinthians 5:7).

APPLY THE BLOOD

I was returning to the police station one evening from a lunch break. We had been having some inclement weather throughout the shift. The rain and the winds grew steadily worse as I approached our station. By the time I entered the station parking lot and stopped my truck, the rain was falling so hard that I could not see through my windshield even though my wipers were switched to their maximum setting. There was almost constant thundering coupled with bluish lightning flashes all around me.

While waiting out what I believed to be the worst storm I had ever been in, I could hear what sounded like a distant train. I had always heard that tornadoes sound like an oncoming train. I thought, *Great, I managed to spend nearly four years in Texas and Arkansas while in the military without ever seeing a tornado; now, in sunny South Florida, I am about to be hit by one while sitting in my own truck.* A vehicle is undoubtedly one of the worst places to be during such a storm.

The noise grew louder and the wind was now shaking my truck from side to side. The leaves and raindrops were hitting the windows with such force that they seemed like thousands of rocks. I pled out loud, "Satan, I put the blood of Jesus over and around me and my truck and I render you powerless and ineffective against me in the Name of Jesus!"

I spoke these words while motioning with my hand in a circular fashion, as if *applying* my protective blood covering around me. (Gesturing with my hand had no power in and of itself, but like the *blood of lambs* and the *scarlet thread*, this served as an overt, physical act of faith on my part. It was a spiritual *token* and point of contact.)

I could still hear the raging fury of what I was now convinced was a tornado. Although my visibility was still zero, and I could feel a rumbling around the truck, the shaking suddenly stopped. As the storm raged on, I found myself in a tremendous state of peace and even began singing a favorite church hymn of mine.

After a few minutes, the rain subsided enough for me to exit my truck. Nearly every vehicle in the parking lot had suffered some type of body damage, and many, including the two cars parked on either side of me, had been moved from their original positions. Every tree in the area had been snapped at its trunk, and the roofs of several buildings were damaged or partially removed. My truck did not have as much as a paint nick on it. Although the hatch on my truck's topper was left unlocked, it was not even blown open. I ran into the station and a buddy of mine confirmed what I already knew I had lived through: "A tornado just hit the city!"

A greater *token of blood* than that which saved Rahab and the Israelites had also delivered my property and me without any sign of damage or injury. I was able to apply the blood of my Passover Lamb in faith because of what the apostle John revealed in his vision of our present-day Church.

> **And I heard a loud voice saying in heaven,**
> **Now is come salvation, and strength, and the**
> **kingdom of our God, and the power of his**
> **Christ: for the accuser of our brethren** *(Sa-*
> *tan)* **is cast down, which accused them before**
> **our God day and night.**
> *And they overcame him by the blood of*
> *the lamb, and by the word of their testimony;*
> **and they loved not their lives unto the death.**
> **Revelation 12:10–11**

The destroyer, Satan, is overcome (conquered, defeated, overwhelmed) by the blood of Jesus and by our words. Just as every other source of deliverance that we have covered in this book is activated—by our faithful confession—so the blood of Jesus is applied or pled. To *plead* is to "state a legal defense."[1]

I have a legal right to use in my defense what Jesus has made available to me through His shed blood. Just as I placed my faith in His blood for my salvation, I confidently trust in and verbally plead His blood for my protection. That is why our tongues can be considered our New Testament *hyssop*. Hyssop was used by the Israelites to apply the blood of earthly lambs to their doorposts (Exodus 12:22). Our tongues speaking the words of our testimony are the hyssop branches that apply a bloodline around us any time we expect the destroyer to come against us in an attempt to steal, kill or destroy.

LIFE IN THE BLOOD

I heard the frantic screams of my neighbor one Easter Sunday morning and turned toward her home. Standing on her front porch with her arms flailing in the air, she desperately yelled for me to run over and help. "My son, my son!" she shouted, "He has collapsed!"

I entered the house and was immediately confronted with an atmosphere of panic and confusion. The woman's husband was also visibly shaken and seemed desperate for someone to help his only son. Lying motionless on the floor beside his bed was a young man partially swaddled in a bed comforter. He was unconscious and did not appear to be breathing. His lips were discolored blue from an apparent lack of oxygen. I felt no heartbeat or pulse. I knew the destroyer was present and was trying to take this young man's life.

Prior to starting any natural means of first aid, I pled the blood of Jesus barely under my breath. I motioned with my hand over his head and upper body, representing the spiritual application of the blood. Immediately, the young man opened his eyes and regained consciousness. He began breathing again and even muttered a few words.

Just as Rahab asked the two spies for the deliverance of her family, I was given the authority to intervene by the young man's mother. Rather than having to use a token, I went straight to the purest source of Passover blood in existence. Jesus' blood is the only blood that makes such tremendous life-preserving power available, and it is the only blood that a New Testament believer needs. Yes, God honored the blood of animals and other tokens of cover in the past, but we have a better, perfect blood sacrifice on which to rely.

> But now hath he obtained a *more excellent ministry,* by how much also he is the mediator of a *better covenant,* which was established upon *better promises.*
>
> **Hebrews 8:6**

> For *if the blood of bulls and goats,* and the ashes of an heifer sprinkling the unclean, sanctifieth to the purifying of the flesh:
> *How much more shall the blood of Christ,* who through the eternal Spirit offered himself without spot to God, purge your conscience from dead works to serve the living God?
>
> **Hebrews 9:13–14**

> And to Jesus the mediator of the new covenant, and to *the blood of sprinkling, that speaketh better things* than that of Abel.
>
> **Hebrews 12:24**

Praise God! The blood of our Passover Lamb is just as alive and *eternally* effectual as the day it first ran down the Savior's side! Jesus' blood is a precious substance that is so *much more* empowered to serve as our source of divine cover than any old covenant alternative.

Like many other Christians, I have learned to apply the blood over and around me without fail. I normally put on my protective cover before leaving my house. During my work week, I dutifully plead the blood over myself and my police car before starting my shift. Unlike a bulletproof vest, the blood serves as divine armor over my entire body. It is an impenetrable armor that shields me from all weapons known to both man and demon.

I also apply the blood whenever I respond to any type of disturbance or priority call that might entail violence or danger. As soon as I arrive on a scene and recognize that the destroyer might be present, I thwart any demonic advances by pleading the blood of Jesus over and around me. I could cite countless occasions when I took advantage of His precious cover and availed over death and injury.

Victory in the Blood

Because of a spiritual attack I experienced one evening, I am able to further explain why Jesus' blood is so wondrously effective against the spirit of death and his agents. I hesitated including the following event in the book, because I felt it might be unsettling to some readers. Then I realized that this was nothing more than a feeble attempt by Satan to keep me from disclosing such a precious truth. Sharing this account will truly convey what happens in the spirit realm when a believer pleads the blood of Jesus.

I was asleep in bed one evening when I began to experience what I initially thought was a disturbing nightmare. I was unusually hot and I began sweating profusely. I felt an extreme, pressuring sensation around my entire body, to the extent that I became completely immobilized. It was as though I had been bound up with a tightening rope from my neck down to my feet.

Believing that the episode would end by awakening, I opened my eyes. I was completely awake but was still paralyzed and under intense pressure. When I looked around my room, I saw shadows of what appeared to be hooded men walking and dashing about. I could hear the murmuring sound of hundreds of voices whispering simultaneously. The shadows then began to rapidly move under and around me in an erratic pattern.

I immediately recognized this as a demonic attempt to frighten and oppress me. I became angry and responded, "Satan, I plead the blood of Jesus over me!"

I had not finished pronouncing the "e" in the word "me," when I instantly felt a refreshing sensation. It felt as though someone poured a liquid substance all over me. The "flow" started at the very top of my head and gently traveled down to the tips of my toes. The shadows and voices immediately disappeared and I regained full motion. The temperature in the room was cool once again. I felt such a sense of victory and so much peace that I leaped out of bed and thanked Jesus for the blood that *He* had just poured over me!

This experience gave me a revelation of why the blood of Jesus is so completely prevailing against the destroyer. The mere mention or sight of the most perfect, sinless, holy substance in the heavens is so overpowering and disturbing to our adversary that he flees in a pathetic state of terror and confusion.

Every time you faithfully plead the blood of Jesus, visualize the fear and chaos you have just handed the kingdom of hell.

> **Through faith, Moses kept the passover, and the sprinkling of blood, lest he that destroyed the firstborn should touch them.**
> **Hebrews 11:28**

Through faith, we too must keep the Passover and the sprinkling of blood. Merely being aware of Jesus' blood and believing in its power is not enough. Applying the blood is what counts. Translate faith into action and the destroyer cannot touch you!

CHAPTER 9

Inside
Information

During World War II, the Germans developed an encoded process of communication that seemed virtually impossible to decipher. Their system evolved around a top-secret machine called the Enigma. Although the Enigma looked like a sophisticated typewriter, it actually sent out messages that appeared as a series of scrambled, meaningless letters to the allies. The letters were prearranged so that an astronomical combination of codes could be used, preventing their interpretation by enemy forces.

The Germans were so confident in the Enigma's invincibility, that they used it to telegraph messages throughout their entire chain of command. Every Nazi field marshal had access to an Enigma and routinely conversed with Hitler and the German high command about top-secret matters and strategies over unsecured frequencies. Because of the Enigma, the Germans could direct their ground, naval, and air forces with devastating results. During the earlier part of the war, they achieved countless victories in every theatre of battle.

Finally, Great Britain decided to do something about the Enigma communication device. The British gathered a group of experts and scientists in a secret, rural, estate home. The sole objective was to break the Enigma's code system.

After nearly eighteen months, the team eventually succeeded in their endeavor. One of the scientists even devised a giant, computer-like machine that deciphered the Enigma's transmissions almost as soon as the Nazis sent them out. Our allies' decoding machine was so efficient that they knew what the German messages meant before they could be interpreted at their intended destination.

Believing that their secret code system was infallible, the Germans continued sending priority messages and commands via the Enigma throughout the war. Soon, the U.S. and British navy knew the location of German submarines and sank them in record numbers. Nazi supplies stopped reaching field units because their convoys were suddenly intercepted and destroyed. German tank and infantry battalions were incapable of making a move without opposing forces knowing about it well in advance.

Having lost all element of surprise, the Nazi war machine's offensive was doomed to failure. Because of our newly acquired early warning system, the tide of battle was irreversibly changed to our favor. The war was drastically shortened and possibly hundreds of thousands of lives were saved.

OUR HELPER

Knowing in advance what our enemies intend to do to us provides us with an undeniable advantage. It is vital to have resources that gather intelligence and in turn give us directions on how to advance against our opponent. This is especially crucial in police work.

Before a raid on a drug house occurs or a major arrest warrant is served, the law enforcement agency involved takes certain measures to collect as much information on its intended target as possible. How many subjects will be engaged? What kinds of weapons are we up against? What is the building's layout? Are there any traps set up?

These are just a few of the questions that must be answered before the encounter can take place. Normally, police Special Response Teams have the luxury of time and surveillance in order to more safely prepare for their missions. Notice I used the words "more safely" and not "absolutely safe." Even the best natural intelligence gathering seldom accounts for every hidden threat variable.

What sort of protection is available for the patrolman on the street or the undercover detective in the field; each going about his daily duties? Do these individuals have resources that can provide them with the early detection of every impending hazard? Is there a system that can also tell us what action to take in order to avoid and defeat the particular hidden danger? Can we access an infallible, all-knowing source of wisdom and guidance that foils the enemy's attacks every time?

If you are a born-again, Spirit-filled, man or woman of God, then the answer is a qualified *yes*!

Before Jesus' departure to heaven, He promised us one such powerful source.

> **Nevertheless I tell you the truth; It is expedient for you that I go away: for if I go not away, the Comforter *(Helper)* will not come unto you; but if I depart, *I will send him unto you.***
>
> **John 16:7**

> **And I will pray the Father, and *he shall give you another Comforter (Helper)*, that he may abide with you for ever;**
> **Even the *Spirit of truth; whom the world cannot receive*, because it seeth him not, neither knoweth him: but ye know him; for he dwelleth with you, and shall be in you.**
>
> **John 14:16–17**

> ...And ye shall receive *the gift of the Holy Ghost.*
>
> For the promise is unto you, and to your children, and to all that are afar off, even as many as the Lord our God shall call.
>
> **Acts 2:38–39**

The Holy Spirit "who dwells within you" is such a Helper (1 Corinthians 3:16, 6:19). The texts in John use the word "Comforter" in reference to the Holy Spirit. The word "Comforter" was translated from the original Greek word *Parakletos,* meaning "one called alongside to help."[1]

The Holy Spirit gives believers a supernatural advantage that "the world cannot receive." As Christians, we are to "receive and be endued *(clothed)* with power, after that the Holy Ghost is come upon *us*" (Luke 24:49, Acts 1:8).

Although the Holy Spirit *empowers* us with many precious abilities as our *Helper*, we will focus specifically on the ones that help to insure our safety. In this case, we will cover the *power* to know, well in advance, whether or not we may be headed into trouble.

SEEING AND KNOWING

Being led by the Holy Spirit is God's *primary* way of keeping us from harm. Every person, saved and unsaved alike, is a spirit being (John 3:6). It is with our spirit that we know right from wrong. Our spirit discerns the "dos" and "don'ts" in our life.

When someone does something that he knows to be a sin or violation of the law for example, he immediately senses what we call *conviction* inside his spirit. He feels *guilty* in his heart and he knows, whether willing to admit it or not, that he has done wrong. This could not be a mental process, because it was an influence on the person's mind that told him to commit the wrongful act in the first place. Guilt is definitely not a physical reaction because the person's body complied with the original mental thought to carry out the transgression. Our flesh and mind desire to do wrong and are in obvious conflict with our spirit (Romans 7:18, Galatians 5:17).

Another role our spirit plays is to actually let us know when something bad is about to happen. Cops and civilians alike refer to this as a "sixth sense." We can probably recall numerous instances when we did not "feel" right just before things took a turn for the worst. "Something" told us that we were about to encounter an unpleasant or negative experience. "Something inside" us spoke up out of our innermost being, and probably screamed, "Look out!" as everything went very wrong.

That "something" was the voice of our spirit, also known as our *conscience*. If a person is not saved and does not have the Holy Spirit's direction, then all his spirit can do is make him feel uneasy or uncomfortable. Our spirit alone cannot tell us any particular detail of what is about to happen. Our spirit alone is also unable to show us the proper course of action to take in order to avoid or defeat what we are about to go through. This is where the power of the Holy Spirit as our Helper comes into play.

> **Howbeit when he, the Spirit of truth, is come,** *he will guide you into all truth:* **for he shall not speak of himself; but whatever he shall hear, that shall he speak: and** *he will shew you things to come.*
>
> **John 16:13**

> **But ye have an unction from the Holy One, and** *ye know all things.*
>
> **1 John 2:20**

Our born-again spirit is the part of us that knows God and hears His voice. When God wants to *guide* us, reveal a *truth* to us, and *show* us something that is coming in the future, He does it by an *unction*: God's anointed voice within our own spirit. Proverbs 20:27 explains: "The spirit of man is the candle of the Lord, searching all the inward parts of the belly." The Spirit of God illuminates or lights our spirit as a candle would light our path. God is a Spirit and can only communicate with the spirit of man (John 4:24).

When we were born again, the Spirit of God came to dwell on the inside of us. Romans 8:16 says, "The Spirit itself beareth witness with our spirit, that we are the children of God." God's Spirit served as an *inner witness* to confirm or bare witness with our spirit that we became children of God. We knew beyond the shadow of doubt that we had gained heaven, and no person on earth or demon in hell could talk us out of our salvation.

John 16:13 says the Holy Spirit will speak to us and guide us into *all truth*. God, as an omniscient or all-knowing Father, shares information of which our mind is not aware. What God knows, we know; what God sees, we see; and what God hears, we hear. That especially includes harmful truths that would have an adverse affect on our lives if we remained ignorant of them. The Holy Spirit "decodes" our enemy's secret plans and intentions and serves as our "early warning system."

LIFE-SAVING INFORMATION

I stopped a suspicious looking car one evening in one of the more seedy outskirts of the city. I could see at least three subjects moving about the inside of the car, but could not tell what they were doing because of the vehicles' dark, tinted windows. The driver seemed to be ignoring my requests for him to step out of the vehicle and walk toward my police car. In a moment of time, I sensed a voice within my spirit say, "The front passenger has a gun; they want you to walk up to their car."

I don't mean I heard an audible voice coming from some exterior source; it was more of a still, small voice inside of me. The message was just as real as if it had been audible. The entire communication was revealed to me in an instant. I didn't hear the Holy Spirit pronounce each individual word; I heard His warning as more of an instantaneous flash or bulletin. It was as if God was conveying several sentences of information to my spirit within the same millisecond.

By the time my backup arrived, the driver had exited his car and was talking with me about the numerous suspensions on his driver's license. While I was dealing with the driver, from the corner of my eye, I saw the backup officer walking toward the subject vehicle's passenger side. I normally don't tell veteran officers what to do or how to do their job, but knowing what the Holy Spirit had *shown* me, I fervently yelled to the officer to stop in his tracks and walk toward me instead. I warned him by using our police codes that there was a gun in the car. After securing the driver in the back seat of my police car, we had the remaining passengers exit one by one.

On the floorboard of the front passenger's seat was a snub-nosed, five-shot revolver. The gun had been reported stolen. Aside from being on probation, the same front passenger also had a felony warrant for armed robbery. He had to have known that being in possession of a stolen firearm, coupled with pending armed robbery charges, were going to violate his probation and put him away for a lengthy, undesirable amount of time. I doubt that the temptation to shoot me and flee did not cross the subject's mind—a temptation that was never allowed to materialize because of my "inside information."

The unction of the Holy One saved my life and the life of another officer. Because I yielded to the voice of the Holy Spirit within me, I changed my course of action and was able to alter the devil's plan to kill and destroy that evening. I thank God for His gentle leading and detailed warning. I also thank Him that my Christian brothers and sisters in blue have the same enduement of power. "For as many *as are led* by the Spirit of God, they are the sons of God" (Romans 8:14).

SECRETS REVEALED

Biblical examples of God's people being led by His Spirit permeate the Scriptures in both the Old and New Testaments. Of particular interest to us as law

enforcement officers are two separate accounts involving divine protection and safety, which led to the actual
deliverance of believers by the Holy Spirit's guiding
voice.

In Second Kings 6, we find that the king of Syria,
Israel's enemy, had set up a military ambush against
the Israeli army.

> **Then the king of Syria warred against
> Israel, and took counsel with his servants,
> saying,** *In such and such a place shall be my
> camp.*
> **And the man of God** *(Elisha)* **sent unto
> the king of Israel, saying,** *Beware that thou
> pass not such a place;* **for thither the Syr-
> ians are come down.**
> **And the king of Israel sent to the place
> which the man of God told him and warned
> him of, and** *saved himself there,* **not once nor
> twice.**
> **Therefore the heart of the king of Syria
> was sore troubled for this thing; and he called
> his servants, and said unto them, Will ye not
> shew me which of us is for the king of Is-
> rael?**
> **And one of his servants said, None, my
> lord, O king: but Elisha, the prophet that is
> in Israel, telleth the king of Israel** *the words
> that thou speakest in thy bedchamber.*
>
> **2 Kings 6:8–12**

Each time the Syrians plotted an attack against
Israel, God warned Israel through the prophet Elisha.

The king of Syria suspected that he had to have a spy amongst his men. This was the only plausible explanation for Syria's failed attempts to destroy the people of God. Or was it?

In verse twelve we read that Elisha *knew the words* that the Syrian king *spoke in the privacy of his own bedroom.* How else but through the Holy Spirit could Elisha know what another man secretly planned and spoke of in the safety of his own castle, hundreds of miles away? Elisha knew the precise location and time of the impending assault.

Although these verses don't provide what other details the Holy Spirit may have spoken to Elisha, I am certain he could have known the exact size of the Syrian force and what paths they were traveling. Had these other factors been an issue, they, too would have been conveyed to Elisha. We can confidently deduce this information based on what we have already learned about our Helper and from many personal experiences.

A SUPERNATURAL WARNING

Aside from my uniformed patrol duties, I served as a Field Training Officer for nearly six years. I was concerned about new officers and wanted to teach them as much as I could about every facet of the job. A good deal of the time I had a new recruit assigned to me during the shift.

Late one evening I was patrolling my zone, when I began to feel tired. I asked the rookie who was with me to drive for a while. He eagerly took my place behind the wheel.

No sooner had we started moving, than I was alerted to a vehicle traveling toward us. It was a Chrysler Lebaron occupied by two males. In an instant I *heard* the Lord say, "That car is stolen. They have just burglarized a second car down the street. A third man is hidden in the back seat along with the stolen property. And you are about to be in a chase."

I thought, *Wonderful: the kind of thing you live for as a cop, and I am not even driving!* The only words I could utter were, "Oh, no!"

The rookie turned to me with great concern and asked, "What?!"

I didn't have time to give him a sermon on the Holy Spirit as my *inward witness*, so I just told him to stop the car. I also warned him that three subjects were going to flee as soon as he turned on our emergency lights.

The situation unfolded just as the Holy Spirit had said: after a brief car chase, all three bad guys were swiftly apprehended within a police perimeter. The stolen car, along with parts from another vehicle, were returned to the rightful owners.

I can recall countless occasions throughout my career when the Holy Spirit *led* me *into all truth* about certain danger. I *heard* His *inner voice* warn me when a dispatched business alarm call was actually a burglary in progress. Oftentimes, the Lord would tell me to request a second officer even if the call seemingly did not need more than one unit. When I arrived on such scenes, sure enough, two people would be in a fight, or some other circumstance would be in progress that required more than one officer to safely resolve the matter.

In every instance, I never heard a loud, theatrical sounding voice, or saw lightning flashing and clouds hovering around me. It was much more like a gentle *leading* from within my spirit—from within my true self (Romans 8:14). The leading was just as real and meaningful as if a red banner with flashing lights was flailing in front of me.

The apostle Paul referred to this leading as a "perception" or "awareness." Paul is a prime example of a New Testament believer who was led by the Holy Spirit. He once boarded a ship as a prisoner of the Roman Empire, and before the ship set sail, Paul received an *unction* from the Holy Spirit that great peril would be encountered on the trip.

> **Paul admonished them,**
> **And said unto them, Sirs, I** *perceive* **that**
> **this voyage will be with hurt and much dam-**
> **age, not only of the lading and ship, but also**
> **of our lives.**
>
> Acts 27:9–10

Because the weather seemed perfect and the seas appeared calm, the Roman centurion in charge trusted the captain of the ship's professional judgment over Paul's *spiritual perception* (verses 11–13): and they set sail anyway. Had Paul not been a prisoner, he would have heeded the Lord's warning and gotten off the ship for his own safety.

A short way into the journey, just as Paul had been forewarned, they encountered a hurricane. The cargo had to be thrown overboard in a vain attempt to save the ship. Once that failed, the crew prepared to abandon ship. After a visitation from an angel, Paul told the men that the ship would indeed be lost, but if they stayed onboard with him, they would all be saved (Acts 27:22).

This time, they were all ears and heeded Paul's advice. Paul's presence on the ship spared every life, but it sure would have been easier for them to have listened to Paul's *inner perception* in the first place. A valuable ship with its precious cargo would have been spared, and a group of men would have gladly avoided a near-death experience.

Because they were not believers, none of the men onboard the ship with Paul were in tune with the Holy Spirit. The Roman soldiers and crew members were guided by the peaceful appearance of their physical surroundings.

Sometimes Christian peace officers are guilty of taking this same comfort in natural circumstances. In so doing we "drop our guard." For instance, when three or four officers are on a scene, we tend to feel a false sense of security and are not as mentally alert as we are when we are alone. We have been taught that such laxness is a tactical mistake, yet some officers choose to ignore this training. If we are not careful, we can disregard the voice of the Holy Spirit just as easily as we discount such teachings on officer safety.

HEED THE WARNING

I recall stopping a car one evening for a minor traffic offense. I was on a well-traveled thoroughfare and the driver did not appear unusually nervous or shaken. He politely provided me with his identification but said that the car's state registration was inside the glove box. He asked if he could go get the registration papers, but I told him I was not overly concerned about it.

A few moments later, another officer pulled up and asked if I was all right. Not sensing any cause for alarm on my part, the other officer stayed in his car while we casually conversed. I was just waiting for the driver's license and history check to come back before sending the motorist on his merry way.

While I was caught up in the discussion with the other officer, the subject said that he was going to find the vehicle registration for me. "Tell him no," the Holy Ghost within me responded.

I ignored His leading and carried on with my conversation. I felt an uncomfortable, almost "sickening" sensation in my abdominal area, or as the Bible says, in my "belly," referring to the very center of man's spirit (Proverbs 27:20, John 7:38–39).

Then, just as the man stood alongside his front passenger door and attempted to open his glove box, I heard a seemingly audible, urgent cry: "Face him and tell him to stop!"

This time, I obeyed and ordered the subject to return to the area behind his car. The man looked at me for a moment, as if contemplating whether or not to comply with my command, and then slowly, hesitantly removed his right hand from inside his vehicle.

At that moment, my police dispatcher contacted me and told me that my subject was a federal fugitive, wanted by the U.S. Marshall's Office. He was a drug trafficker on the run. Search of the vehicle after his

arrest uncovered stolen appliances from a recent burglary. There was no vehicle registration in the car's
glove box, or anywhere else in the car for that matter.
Instead, the only thing I found in the glove box was a
loaded, semiautomatic pistol. The gun had been stolen
in the same burglary as the other property discovered
in the vehicle's trunk. The true motive behind the
man's urgency to get to the glove box was unsettling
to say the least.

My heavenly Father's voice had again served to
deliver me and another officer. Rather than count on
outward appearances and my own soulish abilities, I
have learned to place my absolute confidence in His
omniscient power to guide my every action.

> **Trust in the Lord with all thine heart; and
> lean not unto thine own understanding.**
> **In all thy ways acknowledge him, and *he
> shall direct thy paths.***
>
> **Proverbs 3:5–6**

FINE-TUNE YOUR SPIRIT

We can see why it is so vital for all Christians,
especially those in our line of work, to listen to the
voice of God. To effectively hear from God, we have
to know when He is speaking to us. We have to recognize His voice.

When a person speaks on a police radio frequency, I immediately know who is talking just by the sound of his voice. This skill was developed after months of listening to my zone partners and fellow officers. After a while, I could even tell if the person needed help or backup by the slightest change in the tone of his voice.

The same is true with personal phone calls. Seldom does one have to ask the caller his name once we hear his first few words. If we spend enough time listening to someone, we will know that person's voice.

We recognize God's voice the same way: by spending time talking with Him and listening to Him. *God doesn't talk to me,* you might be thinking. The precious truth is, He does! If we are not hearing God's voice, most likely we are not providing Him the opportunity to speak.

The primary way the Holy Spirit speaks to us is through His holy, written Word. Earlier we explained that God can only communicate with us spiritually. God's words are spirit and they are alive (John 6:63). Every word in our Bible was placed in it by the Spirit of God for our benefit (2 Timothy 3:16). When we read our Bible, God's words literally speak to us (Joshua 1:8). All we have to do is submit to God's desire to fellowship and converse with us daily. The more we read His words, the more we recognize how God speaks and how He expresses Himself. The Holy Spirit never contradicts what the Bible says. When the Holy Spirit says something to our spirit, we will know who is doing the talking and we will follow His voice (John 10:4).

Listening is only half of the communication process; we also have to speak with God. If all we do is sit silently while someone tries to share something with us, it will not be long before the other person takes offense and leaves us alone.

Although God will never leave us nor forsake us, our lack of communication will make it difficult for Him to be inspired to speak with us. The Bible refers to this as "quenching" or "hindering" the Holy Spirit's ability to operate in our life (1 Thessalonians 5:19). It is necessary for us to pray to God and thank Him daily for who we are, what we have, and what He continues to do in our lives. Our heavenly Father wants to hear from us with daily conversation even while we drive to work or mow the lawn. The apostle Paul calls this "communion" with the Holy Ghost:

> **The grace of the Lord Jesus Christ, and the love of God, and the *communion* of the Holy Ghost, be with you all.**
>
> **2 Corinthians 13:14**

The word "communion" in this verse was translated from the original Greek word *koinonia*, which indicates "intimate fellowship and sharing."[2]

God has made so many promises and blessings available to us, and in return, all He asks is that we fellowship with Him. When we speak with God, worship Him, and listen to His voice, we are fellowshipping and sharing in a precious, two-way relationship. As we develop this relationship through daily communion with the Father, we will become sensitive to the Holy Spirit's leading into all truth. It is then that we will be well prepared to hear and heed His inside information! "Draw nigh to God, and he will draw nigh to you" (James 4:8).

Wisdom crieth without; she uttereth her voice in the streets:

She crieth in the chief place of concourse, in the openings of the gates: in the city she uttereth her words, saying,

How long, ye simple ones, will ye love simplicity? and the scorners delight in their scorning, and fools hate knowledge?

Turn you at my reproof: behold, I will pour out my spirit unto you, I will make known my words unto you.

Because I have called, and ye refused *(to answer)*; I have stretched out my hand, and no man regarded;

But ye have set at nought all my counsel, and would none of my reproof:

I *(wisdom)* also will laugh at your calamity; I will mock when your fear cometh;

When your fear cometh as desolation, and your destruction cometh as a whirlwind; when distress and anguish cometh upon you.

Then shall they call upon me, but I will not answer; they shall seek me early, but they shall not find me.

Proverbs 1:20–28

CHAPTER 10

Renew Your Mind

Prior to discovering the wisdom in this book, Proverbs 1:20–28 describes the terrible predicament in which you may have found yourself. Perhaps you lacked the wisdom of God's promises to deliver you from harm. Maybe you knew nothing, or very little, about all the blessings God has made available to you for your protection. How could you possibly partake of such gifts from God if you did not realize you had them or knew how to employ them?

Thank God, you chose not to remain ignorant. God's *wisdom cried out* to you, and you accepted *all His counsel*. When it comes to divine safety, you have now been exceedingly "filled with the knowledge of His will in all wisdom and spiritual understanding" (Colossians 1:9). You have accepted new, supernatural weapons and countermeasures to shield you from fear, calamity and destruction.

In the natural realm, many of us wear a utility belt that holds an array of gear and armament which enables us to carry out our job on the street. We would never consider working a shift without our leather and its full compliment of such tools of the trade. Most likely we have had to depend on each piece of equipment strapped to our belt at least once. (If not, you probably haven't spent enough time on the road.)

The spiritual benefits you have just discovered in this book share a similarity with your earthly arsenal. According to Romans 13, we find that police officers are *ordained,* "appointed, assigned"[1] by the Lord Himself. Three separate times within the first seven verses of the same chapter, God specifically refers to us as His *ministers.*

> **Let every soul be subject unto the higher powers. For there is no power but of God:** *the powers that be are ordained of God.*
>
> **Whosoever therefore resisteth the power, resisteth the ordinance of God: and they that resist shall receive to themselves damnation.**
>
> **For rulers are not a terror to good works, but to the evil. Wilt thou then not be afraid of the power? do that which is good, and thou shalt have praise of the same:**
>
> *For he is the minister of God to thee for good.* **But if thou do that which is evil, be afraid; for he beareth not the sword in vain:** **for** *he is the minister of God, a revenger to execute wrath upon him that doeth evil.*

> **Wherefore ye must needs be subject, not only for wrath, but also for conscience sake.**
> **For for this cause pay ye tribute also: for** *they are God's ministers,* **attending continually upon this very thing.**
> **Render therefore to all their dues: tribute to whom tribute is due; custom to whom custom; fear to whom fear; honour to whom honour.**
>
> **Romans 13:1–7**

God has formidably equipped us for our ministry! Never consider leaving your home or trying to perform your duties without His "gear." It truly is just a matter of time before you will have to call upon and rely on every one of your divine resources. Our heavenly Father would not have made these provisions available to us if this were not the case.

In order to draw your gun or handcuff a subject, your brain has to send a message to the different parts of your body to respond accordingly. Although you will not have to depend on such basic physiological functions, operating in the spirit realm is just as simple. Any spiritual decisions and corresponding actions will occur within your spirit and under the guidance of the Holy Spirit within you. The same Holy Spirit that *helps* to deliver you also shows you what protective promise(s) to reach for. As the situation requires, you will instantly know what scriptures you need to confess, when to plead the blood of Jesus, or when to employ His Name. Oftentimes, you will even be directed to utilize a combination of these blessings.

> **But the Comforter, which is the Holy Ghost, whom the Father will send in my name, He shall teach you all things, *and bring all things to your remembrance, whatsoever I have said unto you.***
>
> **John 14:26**

Because you have *meditated* on the Lord's teachings that cover your deliverance from danger, His wisdom immediately comes out of your heart and mouth in every critical moment you face.

God's words and the verses in this book will speak to *you* and guarantee *your* safety! Your recreated, human spirit now knows to trust God for all of your defensive needs.

TRANSFORMED BY THE WORD

Unlike your spirit, your mind still has to be reprogrammed to accept the things of God, especially many of the teachings in this book. You have just been fed what the apostle Paul refers to as "strong meat" (Hebrews 5:12–14). You might even say you have just received "prime beef"—wisdom that is saturated with optimum quality vitamins and nutrients for your spirit, soul, and body.

You may have been used to diet of "junk food for the soul." Perhaps your mind was accustomed to hearing that you have no control over what happens to you, or that bad things happen to you because God wants to teach you a lesson. Maybe you have heard that God can protect you if He wants to, but if He doesn't, then it just isn't His will.

Such teachings can still be heard in many churches, and yet, everything we have read in God's Word contradicts and entirely disproves these unfounded, "religious" doctrines. The Church in general has strayed from God's true wisdom. God's real thoughts are so much higher than our own that the human brain cannot handle His truth (Isaiah 55:9).

Just like a baby, transitioning from *milk* to the much needed *stronger*, solid food, you might have mentally "regurgitated" some of God's words. An infant, like our minds, has to be consistently fed the stronger food until it is accepted and can affect stout, healthy growth. This is why the apostle Paul tells us:

> **Be not conformed to this world: but *be ye transformed by the renewing of your mind*, that ye may prove what is that good, and acceptable, and perfect will of God.**
> **Romans 12:2**

When you received salvation, your spirit was born again or made new, but your thought processes remained the same. Right or wrong, your mind still wanted to keep doing the things you did before you were saved. You were still conformed to this world's way of thinking and behaving. It was not until you were exposed to God's words through personal study and meditation that you began to think differently. You eventually acted differently and people noticed an outward change, a *transformation*. You lost your desire to pursue certain habits and acquired a greater hunger for the things of God. You desired to partake of and *think* on things that are honest, pure, lovely and virtuous (Philippians 4:8).

The same is true about your thoughts on God's desire and ability to insure your *safety*. Before reading this book, you might have believed that blind fate determined whether or not you made it from one day to the next. Maybe the thought of being a Christian meant barely making it to heaven and not having any assurances while here on earth. Even now, your head might be trying to tell you that some of God's promises are just too good to be true.

These natural doubts do not have a chance; they have to bow to the power of God's Word! Just think of how much more enlightened you are about God's protective plan for your life after having read only one book! Through the Word of God, your mind has begun its *renewal* process. Because God's words are a manuscript of heavenly thoughts, they are producing divine thought patterns in your own mind. His words have bridged the gap between Godly wisdom and your own knowledge.

> **The law of the Lord is perfect, *converting the soul (mind, will, and emotions)*: the testimony of the Lord is sure, making wise the simple.**
>
> **Psalm 19:7**

> **For the word of God . . . is a discerner of the thoughts and intents of the heart.**
>
> **Hebrews 4:12**

Don't stop now. Continue meditating on God's promises of protection and let go of your past doubts and fears. First Peter 5:8 tells us to "be sober and vigilant;" or "think sober-minded." We all know the easiest victim a criminal can prey upon is a non-sober one. Drunks have almost no perception of danger and make the poorest decisions. Their mental and physical faculties are impaired to the extent that they can provide no resistance to attack. They cannot even give officers a detailed description of their assailant.

The moment you start to dwell on or consume anything other than what God's Word says is true about your safety is the moment you stop thinking straight. First Peter goes on to say, "...your adversary the devil, as a roaring lion, walketh about, seeking whom he may devour." When you walk unaware you allow *the devil, your adversary*, to take advantage of you the same way even the weakest thug will easily rob a drunkard.

On the other hand, if you are prayed up and filled up with God's promises, you are vigilant. The devil does not have a chance to surprise you and catch you with your guard down. A Christian who knows his or her identity as a child of the living God and a joint-heir with Jesus Christ is downright dangerous to Satan. A believer who knows what he or she has "according to the power that works in him" is more than a worthy opponent for any and every demon (Ephesians 3:20).

Acknowledge that you are who the Word says you are!

Believe you can do what the Word says you can do!

Say you have what God's Word says you can have!

Don't limit the power of God's blessings with what your head can't totally accept or understand right now. Make a quality decision to continue to seek after the things of God for your own benefit and deliverance. God has:

> **...Set before you life and death, blessing and cursing: therefore *choose life*, that both thou and thy seed may live:**

> **That thou mayest love the Lord thy God,
> and that thou mayest obey his voice, and that
> thou mayest cleave unto him: for he is thy
> life, and length of days....**
>
> **Deuteronomy 30:19–20**

The sum of every decision you have ever made in your past has brought you to where you are today. The choices you make today will in turn determine whether your future is *blessed* or *cursed*. It is y*our* choice. You can continue to conform to the world and take your chances with *death*, or you can *renew your mind* through God's perfect, peaceful words and enjoy an abundant *life*. The question has a simple answer. In His love, God eliminated all doubt and gave us a hint. He tells us, "choose life."

Choose to trust in God's faithful promises of divine safety.

Choose to carry the Word of God as your primary weapon.

Choose to partake of all the power and authority to command deadly forces in the Name of Jesus.

Choose to take your angelic backup on every call.

Choose to live under the impenetrable, scarlet cover of the blood of Jesus.

Choose to listen to the voice of your heavenly Father within you.

Choose God's *Truth* as your *Shield and Buckler*!

Salvation Prayer

As we now know, God's promises of protection are extended to all of His *children*. These promises are contingent upon our "dwelling in the secret place of the Most High" (Psalm 91:1). When we *dwell in Him*—the Secret Place—we also abide *under His shadow*. The Greek word for *shadow* actually means "defense!"

The first step toward dwelling in Him and abiding under His Shadow is taken when we come to know the Lord as our heavenly Father; not just "God," as the world can only call Him. The Word tells us that we can make God our Father by accepting His Son, Jesus, as our personal Savior.

Praying the following prayer is the most important decision you will ever make in your life. By making this confession, you will gain every blessed assurance the Lord has ever made, and of immeasurably greater significance, you will also receive the promise of eternal life in heaven!

Dear heavenly Father,

I come to You in the Name of Jesus.
Your Word says, "...him that cometh to me will I in
no wise cast out" (John 6:37),
So I know You will not cast me out, but You will take
me in, and I thank You for it.

Your Word says, "...if thou shalt confess with thy
mouth the Lord Jesus, and shalt believe in thine
heart that God hath raised Him from the dead,
thou shalt be saved.
For with the heart man believeth unto righteousness;
and with the mouth confession is made
unto salvation" (Romans 10:9–10).

Your Word also says, "Whosoever shall call upon the
name of the Lord shall be saved" (Romans10:13).

Heavenly Father, I am calling on Your Name.
I believe in my heart that Jesus Christ is Your Son.
And I believe that He was crucified and raised
from the dead for my justification.
I now confess Him as my Lord,
and I ask Him to come into my heart.
I thank You for hearing my prayer,
taking me out of this world's system,
and giving me eternal life with You in heaven.
In Jesus' Name, Amen.

Name_____

Date_____

Rededication

God is long-suffering toward us and His mercy endures forever. God's love for us far exceeds what we would consider the limits of His grace. However, if we are honest, most of us know in our heart when we have crossed the line and are out of fellowship with our heavenly Father.

If you are already saved, but feel as though you have "missed the mark," there is good news! No matter how many steps you have taken away from God, returning to right standing with Him takes only one step. In First John 1:9 we read, "If we confess our sins, he is faithful and just to forgive us our sins, and to cleanse us from all unrighteousness." Through repentance, we *turn away* from sin and *turn to* God. Regardless of our sin, if we confess it to God, the blood of Jesus cleanses us and restores us to right relationship with the Father!

Simply ask God to forgive you this very moment. Let the blood of Jesus cleanse you and wipe away the stain of sin. Let today be the first step toward a new life in Christ!

Notes

CHAPTER 1   Ignorance Destroys

1 *Vine's Complete Expository Dictionary* (Nashville: Thomas Nelson Publishers, 1996).

2 *The Random House Thesaurus, College Edition,* 1987.

3 *The Random House Dictionary, College Edition*, 1984.
James Strong, *New Strong's Exhaustive Concordance of the Bible* (Nashville: Thomas Nelson Publishers, 1984).

4 *The Random House Dictionary, College Edition*, 1984.

5 Ibid.

6 *The Thompson Chain-Reference Study Bible, King James Version* (Indianapolis: B. B. Kirkbride Bible Co., Inc., 1988).

7 *The Random House Dictionary, College Edition*, 1984.

CHAPTER 2   True Integrity

1 *The Random House Dictionary, College Edition,* 1984.

CHAPTER 3   Psalm 9*1*1 and More

1 *The Random House Thesaurus, College Edition,* 1987.

2 *The Thompson Chain-Reference Study Bible, King James Version* (Indianapolis: B. B. Kirkbride Bible Co., Inc., 1988).

3 *The Random House Dictionary, College Edition,* 1984.

4 Ibid.

5 Ibid.

6 Ibid.

CHAPTER 4   Power-Filled Words

1 *Vine's Complete Expository Dictionary* (Nashville: Thomas Nelson Publishers, 1996).

2 James Strong, *New Strong's Exhaustive Concordance of the Bible* (Nashville: Thomas Nelson Publishers, 1984).

3 Ibid.

CHAPTER 5   Your Perfect Weapon

1 *The Random House Thesaurus, College Edition,* 1987.

2 *The Random House Dictionary, College Edition*, 1984.

3 James Strong, *New Strong's Exhaustive Concordance of the Bible* (Nashville: Thomas Nelson Publishers, 1984).

CHAPTER 6   The Ultimate Authority

1   Jesus explained, "The highest class of demons you will have to deal with upon the earth are *the rulers of the darkness of this world* (Eph. 6:12). They are just exactly what the Word says they are – they are *rulers.* They rule the darkness of this world, and they rule over those who are in the darkness."

Jesus explained that rulers of darkness also try to rule over believers who are not walking in the light of their redemption, or who don't know or don't exercise their rights and privileges in Christ.

Jesus told me that according to His Word, believers are to take authority over these first three classes of demons: principalities, powers, and the rulers of the darkness of this world. He said that if we on earth will bind the operation of the first three classes of demons, according to His Word, He will deal with the fourth class of demons – spiritual wickedness in high places.

Kenneth E. Hagin, *The Triumphant Church* (Tulsa: Faith Library Publications, 1993), 16.

CHAPTER 7   Constant Backup

1 James Strong, *New Strong's Exhaustive Concordance of the Bible* (Nashville: Thomas Nelson Publishers, 1984).
Vine's Complete Expository Dictionary (Nashville: Thomas Nelson Publishers, 1996).

CHAPTER 8   Scarlet Cover

1 *The Random House Dictionary, College Edition*, 1984.

CHAPTER 9   Inside Information

1 *Vine's Complete Expository Dictionary* (Nashville: Thomas Nelson Publishers, 1996).

2 Ibid.

CHAPTER 10   Renew Your Mind

1 James Strong, *New Strong's Exhaustive Concordance of the Bible* (Nashville: Thomas Nelson Publishers, 1984).

To order additional copies of *Your Shield and Buckler*, for more information on Officer of the Lord Ministries, or to schedule Jorge Diaz for speaking engagements, please contact:

Officer of the Lord Ministries
P.O. Box 246542
Pembroke Pines, FL 33024
(800) 496-6250
www.officerofthelord.com